W9-APD-467

SPORTS ANALYTICS

SPORTS
ANALYTICS

A GUIDE
FOR COACHES,
MANAGERS,
and OTHER
DECISION MAKERS

BENJAMIN C. ALAMAR

Columbia University Press
New York

Columbia University Press
Publishers Since 1893
New York   Chichester, West Sussex
cup.columbia.edu
Copyright © 2013 Benjamin C. Alamar
All rights reserved

Library of Congress Cataloging-in-Publication Data
Alamar, Ben
Sports analytics : a guide for coaches, managers, and other decision
makers / Benjamin C. Alamar.
    pages cm
Includes bibliographical references and index.
ISBN 978-0-231-16292-0 (cloth : alk. paper)—ISBN 978-0-231-53525-0
(e-book)
    1. Sports—Statistical methods.   2. Sports—Statistics.   I. Title.

GV741.A34 2013
796.02′1—dc23

2012047188

c 10 9 8 7 6 5 4 3 2 1

Cover design : James Perales

FOR AMY, WHO IS JUST TOO GOOD TO BE TRUE.

CONTENTS

Foreword by Dean Oliver ix
Acknowledgments xiii

1 Introduction to Sports Analytics 1
2 Data and Data Management 24
3 Data and Information 35
4 Predictive Analytics and Metrics 44
5 New Metrics 65
6 Information Systems 79
7 Analytics in the Organization: Innovation and Implementation 91
8 A Blueprint for Analytic Success 104
9 Building and Managing an Analytic Team 117

Notes 125
Index 127

FOREWORD

Dean Oliver

Sports analytics experts understand that The Game is still human. It is why they got into the field in the first place. It is what all the formulas, numbers, and analyses are about—measuring, managing, and making the most of the *people* who get to play The Game.

That may not be explicit in Ben Alamar's book, but it is implicit. He was a sports fan who was analytically inclined. I was, too. We rooted for teams and players. A lot of people like us wanted to play sports at the highest level but ran out of physical gifts somewhere below that. The passion to do something competitive, to understand and improve on The Game—that kept us watching. The ability to understand data, work with data, and think analytically about sports—that is what created the field that Ben is writing about.

Sports analytics didn't exist as a real job description until long after it was a job for people like Bill James, Pete Palmer, and Tom Tango. They, among others, took to writing about baseball and using numbers to better understand players and tactics roughly in the 1970s. There were other books about numbers in other sports that followed, but these failed to achieve the following of the baseball books. People like Ben read those, learned what to do and what not to do.

The Internet came about in the mid-1990s and allowed so many more people to write, people who may not have had connections to other people but had connections to the world electronically. And many of them had ideas for sports. A lot of sports fans produced websites. A few of those sports fans produced the science of sports analytics that you will see here.

Ben Alamar was an economist who found himself in a fortunate position. That MIT kid who went to Vegas and played blackjack—that was Jeff Ma, and he started up an Internet site when everyone was making gobs of money on Internet sites. His site involved bringing a number of sports minds together to try to build a marketplace essentially for trading fantasy players. He wanted an economist, and Ben was in the Bay Area where all this was coming together. Ben got his taste of sports and how he could apply his economist tools to it, and he found a direction. Though that original company disappeared long ago, it provided Ben with connections and the beginning of a reputation.

He and I didn't meet in the real-world sense for a while after this, but we knew of each other through work we posted online. He applied his tools to data on NBA draft picks. He worked with people on football-player evaluation. And our paths nearly intersected when I left the Seattle Supersonics to join the Denver Nuggets. The person who followed me in Seattle was Ben Alamar. He was part of the organization as they became the Oklahoma City Thunder of Kevin Durant, Russell Westbrook, and James Harden. No one person ever takes full credit for team success—that's part of sports analytics—but Ben was part of important decisions that led to the success of this organization.

Since those early days, we have been rivals and allies, something that happens in the birth of an industry. We competed as part of opposing NBA teams before it was popular to do analytics in basketball. We worked together to build the Total Quarterback Rating that is on much of ESPN's coverage of the NFL—this was at the dawn of sports analytics in the mainstream media.

There aren't many people with the experience to talk thoroughly about sports analytics. There still aren't a lot of classes in it across the country. There aren't a lot of the parents telling their math-inclined children that they can do this as a job. From collecting data, to developing new metrics, to integrating analytics into the decision making of sports franchises, Ben can provide insight on this new occupation. This book is written by someone with great sports-analytics experience for people who want that same experience.

Finally, I should add that sports analytics is not just for people who are already analytical. I have worked with nonanalytical people in the NBA and with ESPN. The "old-school" people who are sometimes portrayed as out of touch—many of them are very smart about the sports they work with, and their feedback into analytics is one of the most important ways to improve analytical methods. The people I worked with on George Karl's staff in Denver sometimes didn't agree with what analytics could tell them. In working closely with Coach Mike Dunlap—now coach of the Charlotte Bobcats—who was very open-minded, I refined methods for evaluating opponents' tendencies, and those reports got more focused and better, found the right questions to ask. That is, in many ways, the value of analytics (in sports and otherwise): they force you to ask more and more refined questions. Those questions do not improve results just for the sports-analytics expert—they can help everyone in the organization find better and better ways to play The Game.

ACKNOWLEDGMENTS

This book would not have been possible without the direct and indirect assistance of many people. Direct assistance from Amy Alamar, Kevin Goodfellow, James Petite, and Shane Kupperman was incredibly valuable. Their input led to significant improvements throughout the process. For their indirect assistance, I would like to thank my fellow sports-analytic professionals, who have been on the cutting edge of this field, helping their teams win games. Most of the examples in this book come from the discussions I have had with other analysts and researchers at places like the MIT Sloan Sports Analytics Conference and the New England Symposium on Statistics in Sports. I have learned a tremendous amount from each of these discussions and am lucky to be able to share some of the insights they generated. I would also like to thank Michael Lewis for both *Moneyball* and *The Blindside*. *Moneyball* directly led to my first job as a sports statistician, and working on *The Blindside* has led to many interesting questions and opportunities for me to extend my work in sports. I would like to thank Sam Presti, Rob Hennigan, and the Thunder organization for being interested in sports analytics and allowing me a seat at the table.

SPORTS ANALYTICS

1

INTRODUCTION TO SPORTS ANALYTICS

The most meaningful way to differentiate your company from your competitors, the best way to put distance between you and the crowd is to do an outstanding job with information. How you gather, manage and use information will determine whether you win or lose.

—BILL GATES

Analytics is a relatively new and rapidly evolving set of tools in the business world, and these tools are being adapted more and more to the world of sports. Analytics includes advanced statistics, data management, data visualization, and several other fields. Because this list is ever changing, implementing an analytics program to gain a competitive advantage is not a straightforward process. Every sports organization faces its own set of challenges in introducing and developing analytics as part of the decision-making process, but understanding the components of an analytics program will help managers maximize the competitive advantage they can gain from their analytic investment.

The push in sports—as in business—to use analytic tools comes from advances in computing power and the availability of massive amounts of data to both teams and the public, which create an opportunity for competitive advantage. Having access to information that competitors do not has a long history of providing teams and businesses with advantage. Teams such as the Oakland A's, Tampa Bay Rays, and San Antonio Spurs have embraced the use of analytics, and all three clubs, though they are in small markets and so have limited resources, have seen tremendous success, in part because of the information edge gained by their analytics programs. The Rays, for example, were one of the first teams to use data from Pitch F/X, which tracks the path of the ball on every pitch to better inform the evaluation of pitchers.[1] Teams that invest in analytic systems and consistently remain on the cutting edge of harvesting information and using analytic tools will gain a consistent competitive advantage over other teams in their league.

Organizations risk realizing no advantage from investment in an analytics program if they do not also invest in understanding and planning how to integrate analytics into the decision-making process. The dangers of not understanding both an analytics program and its integration into an organization were made clear through the results of the recent Sports Analytics Use Survey (SAUS). Twenty-seven individuals representing teams from the National Football League, Major League Baseball, the National Basketball Association, and the English Premier League answered questions on their teams' use of sports analytics. Two respondents on the same team (one in personnel and the other in information technology) demonstrated two completely different perspectives on the availability and application of analytics within their organization (see table 1.1). This is a team that has made some investment in analytics, and the personnel executive was clearly interested in how sports analytics could help his team gain a competitive advantage.

An examination of these different responses demonstrates that even teams that are interested in developing an analytics program face obstacles. These two executives, working for the same, relatively small organization, had radically different views of the state of their team's analytics program. The responses in table 1.1 show some obvious conflicts. Either the IT executive was wildly optimistic about the state of the team's use of analytics, or the personnel executive was simply unaware of the capabilities of the team. In either case, though, what is clear is that the team had not leveraged its analytic investment into a competitive advantage or integrated it into decision making. The extreme difference of opinion in their responses to the statement, "Your analytical capabilities are stronger than your com-

Table 1.1 Survey Answers from Personnel and Information Technology Executives from the Same Team

Question	Personnel	IT
Data is used consistently across all functions (e.g., the same statistics and terminology are used in all areas of the team).	Somewhat disagree	Strongly agree
There is a clear and consistent definition of all information needed about a player.	Somewhat disagree	Strongly agree
The combination of information generated by different functions within the team (e.g., scouting, cap management, coaching) is:	Time consuming	Seamless
The information I need to make decisions is accessed:	Inefficiently	In real time
Quantitative information is used in the decision-making process:	Sometimes	Always
Quantitative information has had a significant impact on the decision-making process.	Neutral	Strongly agree
Your analytical capabilities are stronger than your competitor's.	Somewhat disagree	Strongly agree
There is a clear process for evaluating the analytic personnel.	Strongly disagree	Strongly agree

petitor's," is an obvious sign of missed opportunities to gain a competitive advantage.

The goal of this book is to help teams and other organizations recognize the opportunities for competitive advantage that a strong analytics program can provide. No two teams will use analytics in exactly the same manner. Different levels of investment, long-term strategies, and appetites for analytics will shape how teams implement and develop their analytics programs. Understanding the possibilities of analytics and how to manage them in conjunction with the strategic plan of the organization, however, will give teams the best opportunity to maximize competitive advantage.

Analytics can be used by organizations at every level of sport. How it is used will vary from level to level—high school teams obviously do not have the resources of NBA and NFL teams—but the general ideas and strategies presented in this book are useful to decision makers in all sports organizations. While the focus of the book is on providing information to decision makers at the professional level, there are a host of tools already avaialble for high school and college teams as well. Companies such as Krossover Intelligence and Hudl provide high school and college teams with analytic tools that help them save time and gain insight. So while the main focus here will be on tools for the general managers and coaches of pro teams, anyone connected to sport at any level will gain insight into the potential impact that analytics can have on a team.

WHAT IS SPORTS ANALYTICS?

For our purposes, the term "sports analytics" will refer to "the management of structured historical data, the application of predictive analytic models that utilize that data, and the use of information systems to inform decision makers and enable them to help their organizations in gaining a competitive advantage on the field of play."[2] This definition of sports analytics identifies the three basic components of a sports-analytics program (data management, predictive models, and information systems) and states that the purpose of the program is to aid an organization's decision makers (personnel executives, coaches, trainers, and so on) in gaining a competitive advantage. Putting the three components together with the motivation for the program suggests the framework for sports analytics depicted in figure 1.1.

This framework demonstrates the flow of data through an organization as well as the transformation of that data into actionable information. All types of data first get organized and processed by the data-management function. The data-management function then provides data to analytic models and information systems. The analytic models use data in either a standardized fashion to provide results to the information system or on an ad-hoc basis to answer spe-

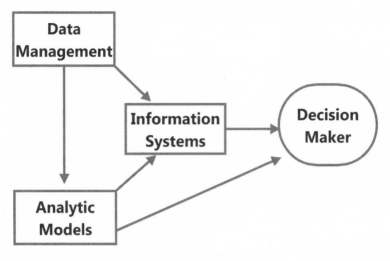

Figure 1.1 Sports Analytics Framework

cific questions for a decision maker. The information system then presents the resulting information to the decision maker in an efficient and actionable manner.

The fourth leg of the analytic table is leadership. Understanding the tools of sports analytics is important to create a competitive advantage, but without leadership that creates an effective analytics strategy and pushes for the use of analytics within the organization, no analytic investment will reach its full potential.

GOALS OF SPORTS ANALYTICS

Building on this framework, the two main goals of the analytics program become clear. First, a strong sports-analytics program will save the decision maker time by making all of the relevant information for evaluating players or teams or prospects efficiently available. Instead of accessing multiple sources of information (such as disconnected databases, one-off spreadsheets, and different departments within the organization), the decision maker finds all of the team's relevant information available in an efficient, integrated, and actionable manner. Good analytics systems provide decision makers time to analyze relevant information instead of gathering it.

The second goal of a sports analytics program is to provide decision makers with novel insight. As the breadth and depth of the available data expand the possibility of gaining useful information from those data grows, but so does the difficulty of finding the information. Analytic models allow decision makers to gain insight into teams and players that are not possible without advanced statistical analysis. Combining statistical projections with the input and insight of scouts, for example, leads to more accurate assessments of a player's prospects at the professional level.

DATA MANAGEMENT

In order to get a handle on the scope of the data-management problem, imagine that every member of a team's staff left the organization except the top decision maker. All of their computers were left behind, so, in theory, all of the data are still available. But how long would it take to access? How much time would be lost in finding the various financial projections, medical reports, and performance data that are key to making decisions? This information is likely well maintained by individuals on their own computers, but is not easily accessed by anyone else.

Next, consider all of the different sources of data that a team has to manage. There is a multitude of data types, including quantitative, such as in game-performance statistics; qualitative data, such as scouting and medical reports; and multimedia data, such as game video. The sources of data are only increasing, and the volume of data that comes from these sources is growing exponentially. In order to gain useful information, the data must first be organized in a manner that allows for straightforward access that is not dependent upon one person.

The role of data management within the analytics program is to organize, centralize, and streamline how data comes into the team and is processed within the team's various functions. It is the principle building block of the analytics program, as the framework in figure 1.1 demonstrates. If key data, such as a team's salary-cap model, are not integrated with the team's other data, then decision makers will have to spend time gathering the information from the person in charge of the cap and the analysts will not be able to combine the salary information with performance data to determine a player's value in an efficient manner.

ANALYTIC MODELS

Analytic models have many uses, but their core function is to turn raw data into reliable and actionable information. Careful analysis takes all of the data, finds meaningful connections among variables, and uses those connections to provide meaningful insight into a player or team's current or future performance.

Many teams across sports use analytic models to aid in their selection of players in their sport's amateur draft. Analytic models are useful in the context of the draft because there is a large amount of data (many previous drafts with known results) and there is a real difference in the level of competition a player will face after the draft. Additionally, the differences in player performances are the result of a variety of factors, such as teammates, system, opponents, and the player's ability to perform at the pro level. Only the ability to perform at the pro level is important to the drafting players, but it can be difficult to separate all of the different factors that affect a player's performance.

NBA teams such as the Portland Trailblazers and Boston Celtics, NFL teams such as the Philadelphia Eagles and New England Patriots, and MLB teams such as the Saint Louis Cardinals and San Diego Padres have all had success using analytic tools to inform the draft process. The Celtics, for example, were able to pick future all-star

Rajon Rondo with the twenty-first pick in the 2006 NBA draft in part because they identified rebounding by guards as an undervalued skill in the NBA. As other teams were picking Randy Foye (seventh to the Minnesota Timberwolves) and Quincy Douby (nineteenth to the Sacramento Kings), the Celtics were able to select a player who would develop into one of the top point guards in the league because other teams did not understand his potential value the way the more analytic Celtics did.

Analytic models provide additional insight into draft decisions by adjusting a player's statistics to make them more comparable. For example, when calculating a quarterback's yards per pass attempt, a good model will adjust the raw data to account for the strength of opposition that the player faced as well as the abilities of his teammates. This adjustment is still just the first step because by itself adjusted yards per attempt is still just a data point. By comparing that adjusted yards per attempt (and other variables) to the data from all the quarterbacks that have been drafted in the past, along with their success or lack thereof in the NFL, the analytic model can turn that data into a probability that the quarterback will be successful at the professional level.

It is important to note that analytic models provide information; they do not make decisions. There are a host of factors that determine how successful a player will be at the professional level. Many of these can be accounted for in analytic models, but it is up to decision makers to weigh all of the relevant information. The goal of the analytic model is to support the decision-making process through richer and more accurate input. Analytic models can be powerful tools in allowing a decision maker to understand a player's potential in a new light.

INFORMATION SYSTEMS

Information systems deliver the information that can be extracted from the data to the decision maker in a meaningful, efficient, consistent, and interactive manner. Information systems organize and present information so that decision makers can spend more time analyzing the information and less time organizing it themselves. Additionally, once an information system is fully implemented every decision maker will be presented with the same information or, as it is known in analytics, "one version of the truth."

When an organization has one version of the truth, then all of the decision makers are analyzing the same information, reading the same scouting reports, and seeing the same video. This kind of consistency allows discussions among decision makers to be less about coming to agreement about an upcoming opponent's actual strengths and weaknesses and more about the tactics needed to handle those strengths and take advantage of the weaknesses.

Information systems also allow decision makers to interact with the information, asking about different player matchups, for example, or how a player's performance can be reasonably expected to evolve from one season to the next as certain factors change. The interactive component of the information system provides significant value over static reports, which cannot present the decision maker all of the different scenarios he or she may want to consider.

A basketball coach preparing for an upcoming opponent, for example, may receive regular standard reports on the strengths and weaknesses of his team's lineups and the lineups of the opponent. In examining the other team, the coach begins to consider using a smaller lineup and faster pace of play. While the coach believes that this will generate more points on the offensive end, he also believes that the defense will not be as strong. Is the gain in offense likely to outweigh the loss on the defensive side? The information system can efficiently provide an estimate of the effects of this lineup against the opponent to give the coach an indication of how big the tradeoff is, which he can then use in discussions with other coaches and ultimately decide whether the tactic is worth using. Without the information system, the best-case scenario is that the coach would have to explain the idea and what he wanted to know to an analyst who would have to do the analysis and then explain the results of the analysis to the coach. Given the extreme time constraints involved in preparing for an opponent, it is unlikely that the coach can do all of that, and so the coach would have to either abandon the idea or explore it without a key piece of information.

Even at the high school level, advanced information systems are changing the way coaches prepare for games and interact with their players. For example, Sean Stokes, head coach of the Stoughton (Wis.) Vikings, uses an online tool that processes all of the game video for his team, creating video edits for his players. What used to take hours is now done almost effortlessly. This kind of advanced information system adds value by increasing efficiency. Coach Stokes reports that "it literally it takes about an hour and a half to download our game and scout film, so our kids within two hours of the final play of our game on Friday night can get feedback on their play." This immediate feedback is highly valuable and only possible through the use of an advanced information system.

ANALYTICS IN THE ORGANIZATION

The two goals of the analytics program (saving time and providing unique information) are applicable to every part of a sports team. But each team is different, and where analytics will have the greatest impact depends on many factors, which will be discussed later in the book. The analytics program, while perhaps initially focused in one area, can eventually provide benefits to every decision maker in the organization.

Coaching

Coaches are constantly pressed for time during a season and are always looking for deeper insight into the abilities and tactics of their opponents. Analytics can help coaches organize in a more efficient manner the information that they use on a regular basis. As video systems have improved, coaches have ready-made edits of opponents to review. These edits are not, however, tied to any player-specific information, so when an NFL coach sees a receiver make a catch down field, he must turn to an alternative source of information to find out whether it was a unique play or if the player regularly makes catches in that area of the field and thus requires more defensive attention. When all the data in an organization are linked together, then the coach can find the answer immediately, without moving away from the video screen. Additionally, analytic systems can automatically detect how an upcoming opponent's performance has been evolving and can identify the cause of any changes. For example, it is straightforward for an NBA coach to see that an upcoming opponent lost six of its last seven games. It is not at all straightforward for the coach to go through each of those games to determine the cause of the losses. An analytic system can demonstrate that each of the losses came against teams that had twice as many three-point attempts from the left corner than they did against other opponents—giving the coach the insight that the upcoming opponent does not defend the left corner well.

Player Evaluation

Standard player evaluation often involves scouting reports, film study, gauging the market value of a player, and projecting the player's role on the team. As the information necessary for the analysis comes from a variety of sources, just getting it together can be a challenging process. Analytics allows for the integration of these information flows. Using analytics while reading a scout's report on a potential addition to the team, the decision maker can efficiently see statistics and video from the game the scout saw, see whether the game was a particularly strong or weak game for the player compared to his average, and see whether the scout's assessment matches his own observations. Additionally, analytics allows the decision maker to consider various scenarios for both the player's role on the team and type of contract offered and so judge a player's long-term impact on wins and salary cap.

Player Development

Decision makers need to identify the areas of a player's game that the player should focus on in her development, determine routines for the player to improve, and provide targets and goals so the player and decisions makers know whether the player is progressing as planned. Analytics can play a key role in this process by assisting decision makers in identifying goals for the player that will best support the team, as well as tracking, analyzing, and projecting progress so all interested parties know whether a player is developing. Additionally, analytics allows coaches and personnel executives to know what the player is capable of achieving in different areas and how that potential fits into the future of the team. Combining the development information with game video, in-game statistics, and scouting reports will further aid decision makers in making decisions regarding the current and future value of a player.

Other Functions

Analytics can assist with all of the functions of a sports organization once the goals of the analytics program are clear. Few if any teams are willing to make the kind of investment initially needed to allow analytics to support all functions, but when a team is initiating or revamping its analytics program, the program should be built with a eye on the future and on supporting the entire team. Many teams, for example, start with analytics by using statistical projections for the amateur draft. This is often a high-value place to begin,[3] but as that capability is being established, the decision makers and analytics personnel should be thinking how the foundation laid in draft analysis will make its way to all other personnel decisions and to coaching preparation, training regimens, medical functions, and financial management. Thinking about analytics in this comprehensive manner allows a team to avoid costly mistakes and establish an analytics program that truly delivers a competitive advantage.

STATE OF THE FIELD

The concepts and the examples used to illustrate them throughout this book are culled from my years of experience in the field and in academia as a researcher and teacher. Many of the examples come from my work with teams in the NBA and NFL. Some examples come from many conversations with analysts, managers, coaches, and other decision makers from a variety of sports, and others, from people who work at companies in the sports-analytics world. While all of the examples used come from real-world applications of sports analytics, many will be described without team and personnel names so that they can be included at all. These examples will be used to illustrate a variety of sports-analytics concepts, as well as the current use of analytics within organizations.

In order to gain the most accurate picture of how analytics is employed across sport, it is useful to first benchmark organizations against the rest of the industry. While it is generally known which teams employ some level of statistical analysis, there is a wide range of sophistication in the actual use of analytics, even in the more analytical organizations. The Sports Analytics Use Survey (SAUS) is the first survey to explore the use of analytics in sports organizations in line with the definition and goals of sports analytics used here. SAUS questions how the different tools (data management, predictive models, and information systems) of analytics are used and managed within a sports organization. Twenty-seven people representing teams from the National Football League, Major League Baseball, the National Basketball Association, and the English Premier League responded to the survey. The responses show that some organizations have embraced all facets of sports analytics, but there is still significant room for growth and improvement and thus opportunity for competitive advantage. Both technical issues and management issues were identified as areas of potential growth for teams' use of sports analytics.

As one of the primary goals of sports analytics is to save time for decision makers, SAUS asked a series of questions regarding where decision makers get their information and how data are stored within an organization. As a baseline, the survey asked respondents how many different sources of information they use on a regular basis (see figure 1.2). Because moving from one source of information to another is time consuming, using high-level information systems to reduce the number of sources of information is an important piece of the analytic puzzle. Among respondents, however, 60 percent use five or more sources of information on a regular basis. The time spent accessing each additional source of information is time that the decision maker can be given back through efficient information systems.

In order to create efficient information systems, data must be centralized, as discussed in chapter 2. When asked about the centralization of data (figure 1.3), only 31.3 percent of respondents reported that all data are centralized, and another 31.3 percent reported that only some data are centralized. Again, there is opportunity to gain a competitive advantage here through better data management.

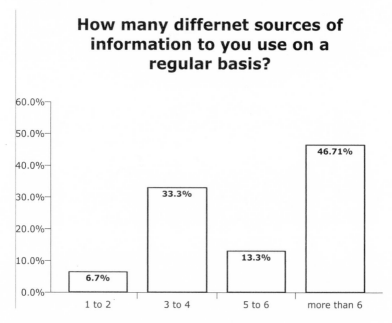

How many differnet sources of information to you use on a regular basis?

Figure 1.2 Sports Analytics Use Survey Results

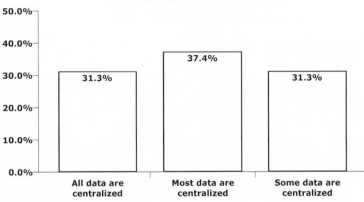

Are data centralized?

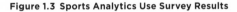

Figure 1.3 Sports Analytics Use Survey Results

Centralization is a building block for efficient information systems, and teams that have not taken that step are wasting the time benefits that information systems can provide.

The opposite end of the spectrum from centralized data is having access to data dependent upon one person. Nearly all organizations report that access to some data is dependent upon one person, and 43.7 percent report that access to most data is dependent upon one person (figure 1.4). This suggests that access to massive amounts of valuable information within an organization is highly constrained. Teams that have invested heavily in analytics and still have data that are not centralized and are highly inaccessible are not maximizing their analytic investment.

As discussed in chapter 2, complex data sets often contain errors, and many of these errors can be identified if not corrected in an automated system. Respondents were asked if data were checked for errors, and only 31.3 percent could report that data were always checked (figure 1.5). Analysis of bad data cannot reliably produce good information, eliminating any competitive advantage gained through the use of analytics. With over 30 percent of respondents answering that error checks happen sometimes at best, organizations are likely relying on poor information for their decision making. Establishing

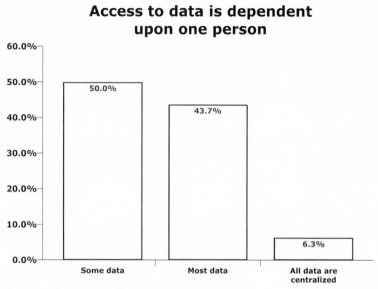

Access to data is dependent upon one person

- Some data: 50.0%
- Most data: 43.7%
- All data are centralized: 6.3%

Figure 1.4 Sports Analytics Use Survey Results

Is data checked for errors?

- Always: 31.3%
- Usually: 37.5%
- Sometimes: 18.8%
- Occasionally: 6.1%
- Rarely: 6.3%

Figure 1.5 Sports Analytics Use Survey Results

clear, automated (where possible) procedures for checking data for errors can significantly improve the information provided to decision makers.

The investment in human resources for analytics is an indicator of how important the use of analytics is to the organization. While technology can be expensive, human resources are a better indicator than purely financial outlay for technology because individual workers require the investment of both time and money. As one of the goals of analytics is to save time for decision makers, adding additional bodies to manage the data takes time. Teams usually commit to higher numbers of analytic personnel only when they see ways to save time in other areas in addition to valuable new information.

Respondents were asked how many database programmers were dedicated to the sport side of the organization. These are the personnel that create and manage the data infrastructure and play a key role in the information systems. Additionally, they support any statistical analysts on staff by providing data sets. Even though this is a central role in analytics, 37.5 percent of respondents reported not having a dedicated database programmer on the sport side of the organization, and only 12.5 percent reported having more than two. As data sets become more complex, the manager of the data becomes more and more valuable. Good data management is the cornerstone of good analytics, and teams can clearly increase their competitive advantage through increasing their data-management staff.

The other component to the analytic staff is the statistical analysts. These personnel are charged with transforming data into information, exploring mountains of raw data to find the meaningful and actionable information. They also play a key role in designing the information systems, working with both the database programmers and the decision makers to identify the most valuable information for each level of the information system, which will be discussed in chapter 6.

Only 20 percent of respondents reported that they do not have an analyst on the sport side of the organization. With 66.6 percent of

How many database programmers are employed on the sport side of the organization?

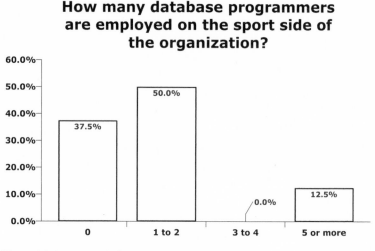

Figure 1.6 Sports Analytics Use Survey Results

teams employing one or two, the information that analysts can provide is clearly becoming an important part of the decision-making process. As a team's data infrastructure improves and the data to become more accessible and integrated, the competitive advantage that the analyst can provide will increase as the analyst is able to create richer and more sophisticated information for the decision makers.

One of the roadblocks to hiring database programmers and statistical analysts is that most sports decision makers do not know how to identify a qualified applicant, especially when first building their analytic team. Once they do hire analytic personnel, decision makers must evaluate and manage them, yet, again, they often do not have a large amount of experience in evaluating the work of database programmers and statistical analysts. As the skills needed are not always clear to decision makers, the quality of the work can often be unclear as well.

The respondents to the SAUS were asked about whether they had a clear process for evaluating their analytic personnel, and the responses support the idea that the management of human analytic resources can be problematic. Only 13 percent of respondents could

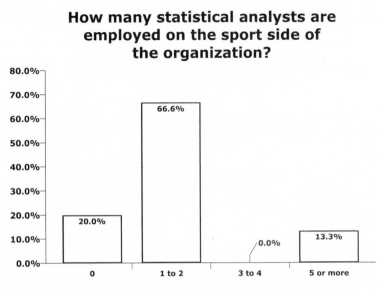

How many statistical analysts are employed on the sport side of the organization?

Figure 1.7 Sports Analytics Use Survey Results

strongly agree with the statement that they had a clear process for hiring analytic personnel, and only 14 percent could strongly agree that they had a clear process for *evaluating* analytic staff. Over 40 percent disagreed with both statements. While these responses are not surprising, they do indentify a path to significant competitive advantage through better recruiting, hiring, and evaluation processes. If a team improves how it identifies, recruits, and evaluates the most talented analytic personnel, then the analytics department will provide decision makers with more time and better information.

Finally, respondents were asked if their analytic resources were in line with the team's strategic plan. The team's strategic plan refers to the long-term strategy for winning games, making the playoffs, winning championships, and maintaining success. Decision makers all have different long-term philosophies and strategies for building successful teams, and it is important that the analytic resources a team employs are established to support that strategy. As analytics is a relatively new function within sports teams, there can be a tendency

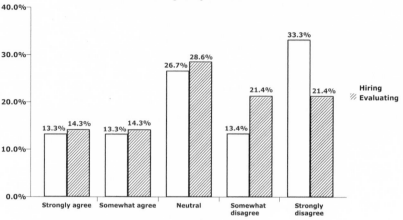

Figure 1.8 Sports Analytics Use Survey Results

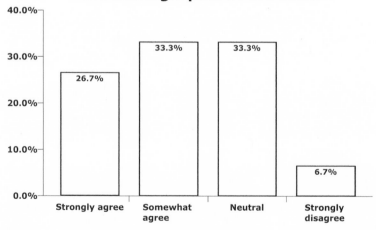

Figure 1.9 Sports Analytics Use Survey Results

to allow analysts and programmers to establish the path forward. This creates a situation in which the analytics group is built up around what the analytic personnel believe is most valuable instead of being organized to support the long-term strategy of the organization. Forty percent of respondents reported that they were either not in line with the strategic plan of the team or were neutral on the topic. Only 27 percent strongly agreed that analytic resources were in line with the strategic plan. The various components of analytics must support (and even inform) the strategic plan in order to provide teams with a significant long-term advantage over their competitors.

The results of the SAUS provide an important window into the current position of analytics in sports organizations. Teams are clearly investing in analytics through hiring personnel and creating more advanced data systems. Since the field is new, however, teams are not always clear on how to manage their analytic investment to maximize return. The following chapters take up this important topic and examine how analytics can be best employed within the organization.

ORGANIZATIONAL STRUCTURES
FOR ANALYTIC SUCCESS

Sports analytics is a tool very much in its infancy. Only a handful of teams are thinking about analytics in a truly comprehensive manner, and fewer have implemented comprehensive programs. This means that there is still plenty of opportunity to gain a significant competitive advantage. Many teams are using some sort of statistical analysis, typically to support player evaluation, and some are using analysis to support coaching and financial decisions as well. Some teams even have good database systems that allow decision makers easy access, but, for example, only 31 percent of teams answering the SAUS say that different departments within the team have easy access to one another's data; 44 percent say that access to some data is dependent upon one person; and, finally, 37 percent of teams do not have a database programmer dedicated to sports functions. But increasing the chance for long-term success through analytics is dependent on having a strong analytics personnel and organizational structure.

Once a team has decided to introduce analytics into its decision-making processes, the challenge is to determine how analytics will fit in an already established organizational structure. There are two basic models that can be used: either a centralized analytic department, in which all of analytic resources employed by the team (both human and technical) are organizationally managed together, or a decentralized model, in which the resources needed by the personnel department are managed by the personnel department, the resources used by the coaching staff are managed by the coaches, and so on. Hybrid models that combine the centralized and decentralized approaches are also possible. Typically, in these organizations the statistical analysts are specialized to a particular function while the data managers are a shared resource. Each of these models has strengths and weaknesses, and there is no absolute prescription for success. Understanding the strengths and weaknesses of each approach is vital to decide which is in the best long-term interests of a particular team.

The centralized model tends to use resources more efficiently as much of the technological investment can be shared among team functions. There is, however a risk with this model, particularly when human resources are low, that one function could dominate to the detriment of others. The decentralized model allows each analyst to focus all of his or her time in a particular area and develop more understanding of its nonanalytic aspects instead of relying on an outsider for information, but that comes at the cost of reducing interaction among analysts—perhaps reducing advances in the analysis. The ultimate model for the analytic program will depend greatly on the resources a team is willing to invest in analytics as well as the willingness of nonanalytic personnel to engage with the tools of analytics. Larger organizations with more resources, such as an NFL team, may gravitate to a more decentralized model, allowing coaches to have "their guy" and the personnel department to have dedicated resources as well, while smaller organizations, such as a college basketball team may, because of resource constraints, employ a centralized model with only one analytic member of basketball operations.

Deciding on how a team can best implement an analytics program to gain a competitive advantage requires understanding each of the three components of analytics (data management, analytic models, and information systems), as well as the structural and managerial issues involved. This book will develop each of the components in detail and will discuss the managerial issues involved, including structuring, hiring, and evaluating the sports-analytics program to maximize competitive advantage. I seek to give any team's decision maker the foundation needed to lead this effort, which will include the hiring of personnel, investments in technology, input from consultants for implementation of some technology, and time to develop the program into an area of competitive strength.

DECENTRALIZED ANALYTICS MODEL (LARGE NFL TEAMS
  → RESOURCES NEEDED BY PERSONNEL
     ARE MANAGED) BY PERSONNEL
  → RESOURCES NEEDED BY COACHES
     MANAGED BY COACHES
  → "THEIR GUY" MODEL

SAUS - SPORTS ANALYTICS USE SURVEY

2

DATA AND DATA MANAGEMENT

Information is a source of learning. But unless it is organized, processed, and available to the right people in a format for decision making, it is a burden, not a benefit.

—WILLIAM POLLARD, PHYSICIST

A general manager for an MLB team was analyzing the pitching staff of the Tampa Bay Rays to identify pitchers of interest to include in a trade. The GM's decision-making process involved collecting data from a variety of sources within the organization to construct a complete picture of each pitcher. The GM requested data on these pitchers from the salary manager, the top scout, and an analyst (among others) and received alphabetized lists of the available data in each area, part of which is recreated in table 2.1.

As table 2.1 shows, each group provided the data in an organized fashion, but because the data were inconsistently organized, each alphabetized list produced a different ordering of the players. So instead of easily joining the data sets together to quickly assemble the information for a complete evaluation of each pitcher, he first had to spend time cross-referencing the lists to pull out the information needed for each player. This example illustrates the need for better data management throughout the organization in three principles: standardization, centralization, and integration (figure 2.1). These three principles build on one another to create efficiencies and consistencies within the organization that allow for easier and more timely access to information. These efficiencies allow decision makers to spend less time gathering and organizing data and more time analyzing it.

Table 2.1 Example of Different Player Names from Different Sources

Salary	Scout	Analyst
Archer, Christopher	C. Archer	Christopher Archer
Brignac, Reid	A. Cobb	Alex Cobb
Bush, Matt	D. De La Rosa	Dane De La Rosa
Canzler, Russ	M. Bush	Matt Bush
Chirinos, Robinson	R. Brignac	Reid Brignac
Cobb, Alex	R. Canzler	Robinson Chirinos
Davis, Wade	R. Chirinos	Russ Canzler
De La Rosa, Dane	W. Davis	Wade Davis

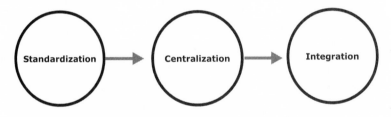

Figure 2.1 Principles of Data Management

STANDARDIZATION

The first step in helping the decision maker work more efficiently is to standardize the data within the organization. Standardizing data and data creation and storage within an organization require knowing the sources of the data. Some data sources are consistent across all teams. For example, all teams use video, keep box-score data, and have scouting reports. Teams also have their own unique data sets. The Houston Rockets, for example, employ a team of game charters that collect data from each game the Rockets play. Many teams are also increasingly employing advanced technology to help collect data around training and conditioning, such as individual heart-rate monitors worn during practice and training and pedometers to monitor the distance and speed a player runs. Still other teams use detailed psychological profiles to evaluate players. All of these data sources need to be indentified in an inventory.

Identifying, locating, and describing all the data sources establishes the organization's data inventory. In constructing this inventory, organizational decision makers need to consider all functions within the organization. Each has a unique set of data that it might create, store, and access in its own way, which, as the example above illustrates, can significantly slow down the decision-making process. The inventory should be used to create a standard set of definitions for the different kinds of data that the organization uses.

The MLB general manager in this example has his time diverted from data analysis to data organization because the names of the pitchers are formatted differently by each department of the organization. The data inventory should include, for each piece of data, a name, a description, and a standard form. Table 2.2 shows an example for a player's name. For each variable, a standard name for the variable is set ("Player"), a description of the variable is stated, and the format for the data in all uses is defined ("Lastname, Firstname"). Now, each department can follow the definitions laid out in the inventory and will enter player names in the same form. The inventory creates a standard throughout the organization so that, even without improvements in the team's data management, the data from different groups is at least more efficiently combined and analyzed.

The process of standardization seems straightforward, but there are actually a variety of areas in which it can prove difficult. Con-

Table 2.2 Data Inventory

Variable	Description	Format
Player	Player's name	Lastname, Firstname

sider, for example, that from 1991 to 1996 there were three players named "James Williams" in the NFL, and two of them were "James E. Williams." All three played different positions for different teams. The repetition of names makes it hard to ensure that the correct player is being identified (to further complicate matters, a fourth James Williams played in the NFL from 2000 to 2003). Additionally, data enter the organization from a variety of sources. Each department uses data from different vendors, and each vendor defines variables in its own way. Additionally, some data are entered by team personnel and some data-gathering projects evolve over time, often starting out as a side activity based on someone's laptop. But these small projects can eventually produce valuable information that is relied upon by many areas within an organization. If the standard definitions are not used as the project begins, then the project must be carefully reorganized when it becomes a significant data asset. Once these hurdles are overcome and data are handled in a standard manner across all functions, centralizing the data becomes possible.

CENTRALIZATION

When evaluating a player, top decision makers often delegate specific data-collection tasks to anyone who has the time to accomplish them. For example, if the decision maker wants to know on what percentage of his team's offensive possessions the prospect touches the ball, the decision maker may task an intern to watch film of the prospect and count the possessions. On most teams, the intern will complete this task using a simple spreadsheet or pen and paper. When any of the decision makers in the personnel department want access to the data, they have to find the intern and request it. Provided the intern is on site and the decision maker has the time, this is not an overly taxing process, but if the intern has been sent to the airport to pick up some prospects that are coming in for a workout, for example, the decision maker may have to wait a couple of hours and delay the evaluation process. This basic example illustrates the importance of good data management and how it can save precious time. If, instead of keeping the information on her own laptop or in her notebook, the intern had entered the information into the player's record in a centralized database, all decision makers would have instant access to the information.

According to the SAUS, access to most data is dependent upon one person on 44 percent of teams, and access to at least some data is dependent upon one person on over 90 percent of teams. Good data management reduces the time spent looking for the people that can give decision makers access to the information they need and provides a team with a significant competitive advantage. When all data are centralized, personnel executives can spend more time evaluating and coaches can spend more time strategizing and coaching—providing them an edge over the competition.

After an organization's data inventory is created and the data are standardized, then a centralization of the data can occur. This makes the data more efficiently accessible to decision makers. The MLB general manager looking for information on the Rays' pitching staff had to contact multiple groups within the organization (salary, scouting, analytics) to get the information he was looking for. The time spent gathering data from different functions diverted the decision maker from analyzing information. When all organizational data are stored in a central location, decision makers can access the information that they need when they need it.

Beyond more efficient access, centralization of data provides additional benefits in terms of data consistency and accuracy. Centralization ensures that all decision makers see the same data. When decision makers are get data from different sources, it is often possible that they see different data even if they are looking at the same variables. For example, if two NFL executives are analyzing the same defensive-lineman prospect for the draft and they each get height, weight, and time in the forty-yard dash from different sources, then it is quite possible that they will be getting different data. While trying to analyze one draft prospect from 2011, a set of NFL decision makers had forty different hundred-yard dash times for one player, ranging from 4.62 to 4.82. This discrepancy could lead to different conclusions regarding the player's prospects in the NFL. While decision makers can certainly disagree about how a player will project to the next level of competition, these disagreements should not stem from having different data. Organizations should determine what the best sources of data are and then have all decision makers rely on the same data.

Having one set of consistent data for all decision makers to rely on is commonly referred to as having "one version of the truth." As discussed earlier, having one version of the truth provides more reliability and consistency and has the additional benefit of saving meeting time for discussing substance instead of background. Once an organization has, for example, defined the set of data needed to analyze an opponent, then everyone attending a strategy meeting can access the information and consider the relevant data beforehand. Instead of spending the beginning of the meeting presenting the data, everyone already has had access to "the truth," and the substance of the meeting can begin immediately. This efficiency gives coaches more time to discuss and analyze (both at the meeting and in preparation for the meeting), which provides the team with a competitive advantage.

Centralization also allows higher-quality data. Errors in organizational data are a significant problem in general; a recent survey found that approximately 59 percent of spreadsheets used for significant business practices contain errors.[1] Additionally, when asked in SAUS, only 31 percent of respondents said that data are always checked for errors before being used in the decision-making process. The high quantity of errors in spreadsheets and the lack of error checking suggest that data quality is a problem that virtually every organization faces, yet surprisingly little thought is put into solving the problem.

No matter how sophisticated and thorough a decision-making process is, it will not be successful if the input (the data) is faulty. When teams use more complex data sets, such as play-by-play data or even

Table 2.3 Example of Play-by-Play Data

Offense	Defense	Play type	Player	Yards	Down	To go
JAC	BUF	rush	28-F.Taylor	0	1	10
JAC	BUF	pass	7-B.Leftwich	12	2	10
JAC	BUF	pass	7-B.Leftwich	0	3	8
BUF	JAC	pass	11-D.Bledsoe	8	1	10
BUF	JAC	rush	20-T.Henry	5	2	2

motion-capture data, identifying the errors in the data is even more a prerequisite for accurate analysis. One example of a common data error can be seen in table 2.3, which is an example of NFL play-by-play data. In this example, Jacksonville gains no yards on first and ten to create a second-and-ten situation. According to the data, they then rush for twelve yards on second and ten, yet the next play is third and eight. In this situation, either the down and yards to go are incorrect, the yards gained on second and ten is incorrect, or some event occurred that was not captured in the play by play. Examining the next few plays, it appears that it is the yardage gained that is incorrect, as Jacksonville gains no yards on third down and then Buffalo takes over.

Allowing this error to go unchecked could lead to incorrect calculations about Jacksonville's yardage gained for the game, per pass attempt, and in second-and-long situations. But a basic error-checking process can, at the very least, identify the inconsistency. And, in many cases, this type of error can be automatically corrected. Once all organizational data are centralized, the problems associated with faulty data are reduced in two ways: only the best and most reliable sources of data are used, and consistent error-checking processes can be put in place.

INTEGRATION

Once the data has been standardized and centralized, it can be fully integrated. The integration of data across functions within the organization allows for seamless access to every department's data. Scouting and medical reports are linked to play-by-play data, which are linked to video files, and the connections go on. On its own, each type of data is valuable, but when integrated, there are synergies created among the different data sources that cannot occur when the data are segregated.

One of the key areas of synergy from data integration is injuries. All decision makers in sports worry about injuries because they are to some degree uncontrollable and their impact on an athlete's career is not well understood. Executives such as Houston Rockets general manager Daryl Morey and Dallas Mavericks owner Mark Cuban have asked very publically about how data can be better used to understand injuries (both prevention and effect). That type of analysis could include data from training staffs and coaching staffs, performance data, and medical data. While most of the necessary information for this type of analysis exists in most pro sports organizations, merely assembling and organizing all of the data is a monumental task because of the lack of centralized and integrated data systems. While the information such an analysis could produce is highly valuable, such wide-ranging historical studies are rarely done in sports organizations because of the massive coordination effort needed to simply get the data in a form that can be analyzed.

The MLB general manager who was trying to analyze the Rays' pitching staff knew that he needed the three different data sets in order to make a decision. He requested salary data, scouting reports, and analysis from the analytics group. Once it was delivered, he had to go through the process of merging the information presented to him. In his case, it involved reading each report separately and cross-referencing, getting the distinct point of view from each department. However, if the data were integrated, all the information could be delivered in one cohesive report. That report could present the relationships among the different data sources, highlighting discrepancies among the various points of view of each function. Presenting the data in this integrated fashion allows the decision maker to identify and explore the differences of opinion in a more efficient manner. For example, if the analytic data paint a different picture of a player from the scouting reports, integrated medical information may be able to explain the differences. If medical data do not explain, then integrated video lets the GM see the player in action and decide for himself which information is most relevant. The integration of data means that all of the different types of information are presented together for a complete picture.

The three components of data management discussed here (standardization, centralization, and integration) provide a basis for an efficient data-management system that will provide a competitive advantage by saving time for decision makers and creating a more complete picture of the team or player being analyzed. With an efficient and consistent data-management system, the decision-making process no longer involves opening a variety of spreadsheets and other documents as well as making a series of calls to get the necessary data. All of the information is available when the decision maker is ready to begin, and it is less likely that a piece of the information will be missed because the right person was not available to produce to it in a timely manner.

STANDARDIZATION → CENTRALIZATION → INTEGRATION

IMPLEMENTATION

The value of strong data management that uses standardization, centralization, and integration is fairly clear. The implementation of these concepts can be more complex, however, because it requires both investments in technology and change in the behavior of all the members of the staff. In order to move from a culture of data silos to a centralized system, the whole organization needs to understand the importance of the new data-management system.

The investment in data-management technology is the first step and can be accomplished either through hiring a staff to build the data system, hiring consultants to build the system, or purchasing software "off the shelf." The Cleveland Indians and Seattle Supersonics both used full-time staff members to build their data-management systems. The system that Keith Woolner built in Cleveland prompted one user, who began his career in Cleveland and then moved to another team, to say that it had "totally spoiled us, the questions we could ask [in Cleveland] and get quick answers to were amazing, we have nothing even close to that here." The success in Cleveland was largely attributable to Woolner's focus and his development of the support staff around the system. Though the Supersonics started down the same path as the Indians, the results were different.

In 1998 the Supersonics hired an engineer named Rich Cho, who had a law degree and a passion for sports. He was charged with building a state-of-the-art database system. Cho's system was a leap forward, but the team had found an asset in Cho, who quickly moved up the ladder in the personnel department. This left the system to stagnate as the team did not hire any staff to continue its development. By the time the team hired Sam Presti as general manager in 2007, the system was not Cho's priority and had not advanced much since its original build. The Supersonics, who would become the Oklahoma City Thunder in 2008, were left with a system that needed to be either completely overhauled or replaced. The Supersonics' experience demonstrates that the data system, whether initially built by in-house staff or consultants, must be seen as an ongoing process, not a one-time investment, and staff must be available to work on the system so it remains up to date.

Once the system is in place, there must be a strong push from management to pressure departments and individuals to give up control of their data and allow it to be shared across the organization. Management needs to establish clear guidelines as to how and where data is to be stored so that the full value of the investment can be achieved. This can be a difficult transition; because of habit and a desire to control, some staff members may find it hard to change their work flows. One NFL team established a system that included having coach's reports from practice sent directly into the system so that the information was available to the entire coaching staff and personnel department. The general manager quickly discovered that the reports were not coming in from the defensive coaching staff. Thinking initially that there might be some kind of technical issue, the GM asked the head coach about it. The head coach asked the defensive coordinator and was informed that "if that SOB wants my input, he can come ask for it." While this anecdote may point to some deeper organizational dysfunction, it also shows leadership's role in establishing compliance with the new technology. In order to avoid this kind of problem, the benefits, in terms of saving time and free access to data, need to be made clear to all users. Once all data are centralized, all users need to be educated carefully on how to use the system and why it should be used. Once staff members realize that using the centralized data system actually saves them the time and headache of tracking down data, they are far more likely to embrace it.

ADDITIONAL RESOURCES

The concepts of data management that are presented in this chapter largely emerge from the work of those in the data-warehousing field. This is well developed in some industries, and information on it can found in the following texts and resources:

Hoberman, Steve, Michael Blaha, Bill Inmon, and Graeme Simsion. *Data Modeling Made Simple: A Practical Guide for Business and IT Professionals* (Bradley Beach, N.J.: Technics Publications, 2009).

Inmon, William H. *Building the Data Warehouse*. 4th ed. (Indianapolis, Ind.: Wiley, 2005).

Berson, Alex, and Larry Dubov. *Master Data Management and Data Governance*. 2nd ed. (New York: McGraw-Hill, 2010).

Corr, Lawrence, and Jim Stagnitto. *Agile Data Warehouse Design: Collaborative Dimensional Modeling, from Whiteboard to Star Schema* (Leeds: DecisionOne Press, 2011).

3

DATA AND INFORMATION

It is a capital mistake to theorize before one has data. Insensibly one
begins to twist facts to suit theories, instead of theories to suit facts.

—SIR ARTHUR CONAN DOYLE

As a high school wrestler preparing for a championship match in
a two-day-long tournament, I was approached by a coach from
another school. His school was a major rival of my opponent's school,
and my opponent had beaten his wrestler in my weight class in the
semifinals. He offered me some advice about my opponent. It seemed
that every time this coach had seen him starting from a standing position during the tournament, my opponent took two steps to his
left as the whistle blew to start action.

Was this useful information? At the time I believed it to be and at-
tempted to take advantage at the first whistle. I made a move toward
where my opponent would move. Unfortunately for me, he was not
there, and six minutes later I was the silver medalist. The truth is,
however, that what the other coach had told me was not information
at all but rather some raw observational data. Raw data are rarely
useful because data are just an input, with no analysis or context.
What this coach had provided was data that in a series of maybe two
or three matches my opponent had taken a particular action in a particular situation. While this could potentially be part of an analysis
of the opponent's tendencies and be incorporated into useful information, by itself it is fairly worthless because it has no context. How
many times did the coach actually see this occur? Who was the

wrestler wrestling against and what were his opponents' strengths and weaknesses? Did the other wrestlers employ a similar style to my own? All of these and many other questions need to be answered in order to transform the coach's data into useable information.

Scouting reports by their very nature are raw data and nothing to base a decision on. For example, if a scout had attended an NBA game on November 3, 2010, he would have seen Kevin Durant take ten three-point shots against the Los Angeles Clippers and hit none of them. This raw data, if treated like information, would suggest that Durant was a lousy shooter and an inefficient scorer because he was wasting so many of his team's possessions by taking shots he obviously could not make. If, however, those observations were treated as raw data and the player was evaluated in a larger context that included more games, the player's age, the opponents faced, and so on, a decision maker would see that the player taking those shots actually shot 36 percent from beyond the three-point line that season outside of that game, led the league in total scoring, and was one of the most efficient scorers in the league, averaging more than 1.4 points per shot attempt.

Before diving deeper into the difference between data and information, however, a clear understanding of data and the various types of data is needed. The word "data," particularly in the context of analytics, is often associated with quantitative data. Quantitative data, however, is just one type of data that is used on a daily basis by decision makers. Along with quantified data such as box scores and draft-combine results, decision makers use a host of qualitative data. Qualitative data take a variety of forms, including scouting reports, coach's notes, and video. Understanding the basic nature of the different types of data is fundamental to being able to see a clear distinction between data and information.

QUANTITATIVE DATA

It is easy to believe a number because it appears to be a fact, something indisputable. The problem, however, is that quantitative data are just data, the lowest input into the analytic process, and without being transformed into information, they are at best useless and can often be misleading. Just because data are presented in the form of an average or a percentage or a ratio does not mean that it is useable information.

At the MIT Sloan Sports Analytics Conference in 2011, Stats LLC, which is a sports-data company, demonstrated its cutting-edge SportVu data service. SportVu involves a system of six stationary cameras positioned over a basketball court (similar technology is also employed in baseball and soccer), and these cameras track every moving object on the court. The system creates a large data file for each game, which provides the location of every player and the ball twenty-five times every second. For a forty-eight-minute game that is 72,000 observations or 5.9 million observations per team per season. These data in isolation are clearly useless; no one can look at the millions upon millions of rows raw data and glean anything meaningful from them. Some processing of the data is in order.

Stats LLC did process some of the data and calculated Kevin Durant's shooting percentage when he dribbled the ball three or more times and when he dribbled the ball two or fewer times. Comparing the two averages, it appeared that Durant's shooting percentage roughly doubled when he dribbled the ball two or fewer times. Stats LLC's goal in presenting this information was not to present detailed scouting information on Kevin Durant but rather to demonstrate the capabilities and potential of their system. One NBA executive remarked that this data point could be used against Durant and his team, suggesting that the data from Stats LLC were somehow useable information.

Unfortunately, the executive's perception of these data as actionable "facts" puts far too much confidence in numerical data. The inference that the executive made was that if opponents forced Durant to put the ball on the floor and dribble more, then his scoring ability would drop significantly. Treating Stats LLC's "fact" as data (as it was intended) allows us to see that it could prove to be useful but has not reached the point of being actionable information. What were the distances of the shots in the two averages? Perhaps the shots that came after two or fewer dribbles included more fast-break dunks and put-backs. If Durant dribbled less because he was more often on the wing on a fast break and simply took a pass and dribbled once on the way to dunking, then comparing that shooting percentage to when he was creating a shot for himself on the perimeter is meaningless: the two averages measure entirely different skills.

The lesson here is that numerical data are not meaningful on their own. Raw data do not provide a decision maker with actionable information because they have no context. Only after raw numerical data are given rich context do they become information that can be used in the decision-making process. It is important not to be tricked into seeing numerical data as information just because someone has put numbers in front of you.

QUALITATIVE DATA

Team front offices tend to separate qualitative data from quantitative data. Scouting reports, medical reports, video, and other sources are all kept in discrete locations and not combined with quantitative data. In part, this is because of the nature of qualitative data. Most qualitative data are what is known as unstructured data, which means there are no distinct variable names and the data cannot not be easily and logically put into a set of rows and columns in a spreadsheet. Some organizations use structured reports for scouting in which scouts enter specific data into specific fields, and these can be stored in much the same way as quantitative data. But even these often include some sort of unstructured written narrative. When data take the form of words or images, though, we tend think about and process them differently than we do with quantitative data.

The result of this distinction is the situation depicted in figure 3.1. Here, the decision maker is getting information from a variety of sources, and analysis is disjointed. The benefits of the centralization and integration of structured data are greatly reduced. Additionally, each kind of data is analyzed separately; there is no point in the pro-

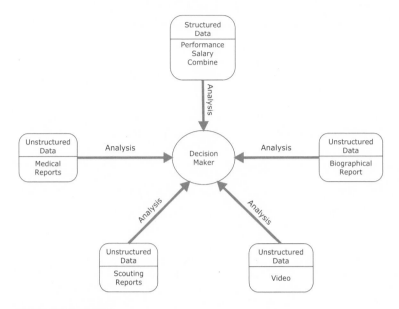

Figure 3.1 Data Silos

cess where the different types of data and analysis can inform one another.

Because qualitative data can be unstructured, the differences in handling and processing this kind of data are natural, but this does not mean that quantitative and qualitative data should be strictly segregated. Raw qualitative data are no more meaningful than raw quantitative data, and they, too, need to be processed and transformed into useable information. For example, a scouting report from one game may produce several pages of notes—raw data. Before these quantitative data can be useful, they need to be combined with other scouting reports, medical reports, video edits, and other kinds of data that the organization uses.

The general attitude toward qualitative data leads organizations to store them in a more careless manner. It is not uncommon for some of an organization's most important qualitative data to reside only on the computers of a few individuals. Medical data, for example, are rarely organized and stored with the same care and structure as salary data. Often the medical staff is the sole arbiter of where and how those data are stored and who may access it. This means most medical data are left unstructured and are rarely turned into useable information. That this type of careless data management creates problems is clearly evident through the general lack of understanding of the long-term effects of injuries on performance. The data that could be used to establish those effects exist in virtually every sports organization, yet it never happens because of the nature of the data. In order to maximize the return on analytic resources, all data should be centralized so that it can be processed, turned into useable information, and accessed efficiently.

ANALYSIS OF UNSTRUCTURED DATA

The transformation of qualitative data has been typically performed through manual processing. This can take the form of viewing and tagging video to create edits for coaches and other decision makers, reading and summarizing scouting reports, and reading and "clipping" related articles. This type of processing has been made somewhat more efficient through improved technologies (video-editing software, the Internet, and so on), but these unstructured data sets still often require a significant investment of time in order to create useful information from them. It is possible, though, to impose structure on these unstructured data in order to reduce the processing time. New technologies that cull information from unstructured data sets can also be used to assist in the transformation of the unstructured data into useful information.

Imposing structure on unstructured data sets makes the information more easily harvested from the data. For scouting reports, creating a more standardized report that asks for specific grades or ratings in particular areas while still preserving a more free-form comments section can make summarizing that data more efficient and easier to incorporate with other types of information. For video data, this can take the form of using play-by-play data or the motion-capture data to make finding, gathering, and organizing specific types of plays or situations more efficient.

The potential downside to imposing structure is that some of the finer points may be squeezed out of the data. A scouting report that is too structured, for example, may not capture some important data from a player's performance for which there is no structured field. For example, if a player appears to be playing with an injury, a completely structured report may have a check box for injury or even the apparent severity of the injury, but if the scout then hears from a member of the training staff that the player was out partying too late the night before and that while the injury is not a fake, it is not as severe as it appears, there may be no way for the scout to convey that data in the report. These nuances can be important; thus, when designing the data structure, allowing for flexibility is important. Additionally, even if the data are completely unstructured and there is no apparent method for creating a structure, there is a growing set of statistical tools that can process massive amounts of text or other unstructured data and pull out useful information. These tools identify patterns within the text and can then use those patterns in combination with other data to create valuable information. For example, if a series of scouting reports on a player seem to be contradictory, text analytics can identify positive and negative reports and then use the data from those reports to compare the scouting reports to information from the games, such as start time, weather conditions, home/away, or other factors. If, for example, the majority of the negative reports are from games with early start times while the games with positive reports have later start times, then important information has been created through the combination of structured and unstructured data sets.

TEXT ANALYTICS FOR QUALITATIVE DATA
→ IE SCOUTING REPORTS

DATA INTEGRATION REVISITED

The combination of structured and unstructured data sets into usable information is only possible when the data are centralized and

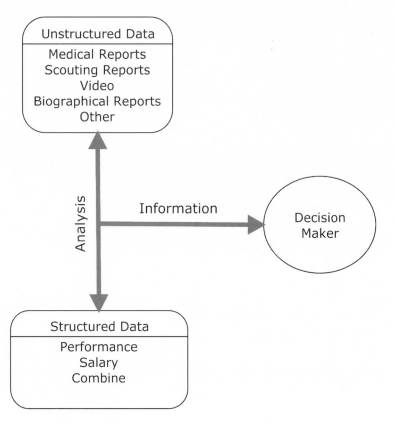

Figure 3.2 Data Integration

fully integrated. Centralization allows an analyst to access the relevant data efficiently. The integration of data discussed in the previous chapter allows for the processing of the data sets jointly in an efficient, easily repeatable (potentially automated) fashion. This results in the situation depicted in figure 3.2, in which the different types of analysis of the various data types within the organization inform one another, presenting one rich set of information to the decision maker.

Just as raw quantitative data inspire questions, so, too, does raw qualitative data. Very often it is the combination of the two data types that allows the data to become information. The combination may be a simple presentation of the two kinds of data together so that the decision maker sees all of the information at the same time, or it may be the joint analysis of the data sets that creates a unique new set of information for the decision maker. Meshing different types of data to create unique information is particularly valuable in the creation of new metrics, which is discussed in detail in the next chapter. Either way, as discussed in chapter 2, centralization and integration of the data are necessary to maximize the useable information extracted from the data.

4

PREDICTIVE ANALYTICS AND METRICS

Prediction is difficult, especially about the future.

—YOGI BERRA

The United States Olympic Committee faces a very specific task: win as many medals as possible in each and every Olympics. This task is made particularly difficult by the limited financial resources that the USOC can use to support the American Olympic athletes. Therefore, the USOC must make sure that it invests only in athletes with a realistic opportunity to win medals. The decision makers at the USOC must regularly ask whether spending the next $1,000 on athlete A is more likely to yield a medal than spending it on Athlete B, even if those two athletes compete in different sports or even in different years. Because of the complexity of multiyear planning and cross-sport comparisons, analytic models have proven to be very helpful in informing these decisions.

Consider a case in which the committee is assessing the progress of a seventeen-year-old sprinter. As sprinters generally compete at the Olympic level in their early to mid-twenties, the decision makers at the USOC must assess the likelihood that this sprinter will be able to compete at a medal-winning level in five to seven years. The decision makers must examine the athlete's record of achievement to determine whether she or he is on the medal-winning path. For example, if the sprinter ran the hundred-meter sprint at 12.1 seconds in competition at age fifteen and now runs it in 10.3 seconds, is she on course to have a medal-winning time in either of the next two Olympic games? With no analysis, the committee has to rely on the opinions of experienced coaches and others involved in the sport. While this input is certainly valuable, it does not leverage all of the information available. By using historical data as well as the sprinter's own performances at sanctioned competitions, a complete picture of the sprinter's progress can be created and analyzed.

The first step is to determine what a medal-winning time will be in five to seven years. Olympic times in the hundred-meter sprint, for example, have continued to drop,[1] which means that the bar is ever higher for developing sprinters to have a legitimate opportunity to win an Olympic medal. Using data from international competitions over the last forty years allows the USOC to project how the likely medal time will change over the next five to seven years. This projection provides the context that the decision makers need in order to assess the Olympic prospects of a young sprinter.

The next step is to estimate the sprinter's progress. Data from competitions can be used to estimate this over the next several years. Figure 4.1 combines the various elements of the sprinter's prospects into a complete picture. In this analysis, the actual competition

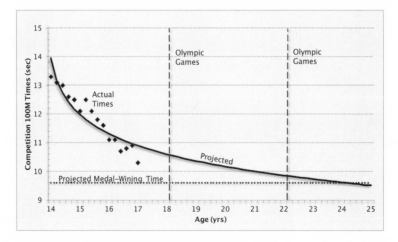

Figure 4.1 Sprinter's Projected Progress by Age

times are represented by diamonds, the sprinter's estimated time by age is represented by a solid line, the timing of the Olympic Games is marked by vertical dotted lines, and the projected medal-winning time is represented by the dotted horizontal line. The figure demonstrates that at the time of the next Olympics, the sprinter will be just over eighteen years old and will be likely running the hundred-meter sprint in approximately 10.6 seconds. The projected medal-winning time is well below that, indicating that the sprinter will not be ready to compete in those games. The following Olympics will occur when the sprinter is twenty-two. By this time she is likely to be running a sub-ten-second hundred meters but still not quite fast enough to be in medal contention. The decision makers at the USOC now have evidence to suggest that the sprinter is not on track to win a medal in the next two Olympic Games and must allocate their resources accordingly. The use of resources is now a strategic decision; the decision makers can either cut funding to the sprinter or, if they do not have better alternatives, closely examine the sprinter's training program and suggest changes so that she or he may get on a medal-winning path.

ASKING THE QUESTION

Perhaps the most important attribute for a decision maker in aiding the development of an analytics program is the ability and willingness to ask questions. While it is incumbent on the analysts to provide clear and usable analysis, their ability to do so is greatly enhanced when decision makers ask questions not about the analysis but about the decisions that they have to make. Analysts bring a set of skills and often a fairly sophisticated view of the sport to the table, but rarely will the analyst understand the sport as deeply as the top decision makers. With that in mind, decision makers need to ask questions based on their deep knowledge of the sport with the goal of gaining some additional insight either into the sport in general or about a specific player or team.

Some questions, those that usually prove to be the most interesting, never get asked because the decision maker does not believe that the answer can be quantified. These questions are usually not unquantifiable but just have not been previously quantified. In the area of player evaluation, these are often referred to as the player's intangibles and come in a variety of forms in a nonquantitative scouting report:

PLAYER INTANGIBLES

- Makes his teammates better
- Great leader
- Hustles on every play
- Coachable

Comments such as these are often viewed as squarely in the domain of unquantifiable player attributes, so questions about measuring these attributes and how they affect a player and his team's performance go largely unasked. If decision makers instead begin to ask the questions and probe on the meaning and effect of these attributes, the analyst can often devise methods to measure what was previously unmeasured—not immeasurable.

One example of this is the effect of teammates on one another. Some teams seem to play above what the sum of their parts suggest, and this ability not only to play well but to play well together is often referred to as team chemistry. The theory goes that some teams have good chemistry and thus teammates raise one another's games, and others do not and so underperform. The concept of team chemistry is regularly discussed as an important but immeasurable trait. However, it is not precisely defined so the term can carry slightly different meanings to different people. Dean Oliver (author of *Basketball on Paper* and analyst for the Seattle Supersonics, Denver Nuggets, and ESPN) started to ask sports executives and coaches what they meant when they referred to "chemistry" in an effort to measure it. Several themes emerged, so Oliver approached this question with the idea that athletes have specific skill sets and that some skill sets fit together better than others. Simply by starting to ask the questions and building basic models around how teammates might actually make one another better, he was able to develop an approach to quantifying how well teammates fit.[2] Oliver's work on teammate fit was not a comprehensive answer to the question of team chemistry, but it is a starting point that helps measure and explain an important concept in sports that was previously unmeasured. This is just one example of how attributes previously thought to be intangible can at least begin to be measured when the right questions are asked.

In order to fully embrace asking questions, it is important for decision makers to have a clear idea of what it means to measure or quantify something. Putting a number on a skill, for example, often denotes a level of precision that is simply false. The goal of quantifying something, hitting ability in baseball, for example, is not to know beyond a shadow of a doubt exactly how good a hitter a particular player is, but rather to reduce the uncertainty around the decision maker's evaluation of the player's hitting ability. The evolution of batting statistics is a good example of the idea that we are not measuring anything exactly but rather are using the information we have to get as clear a picture as possible about a player's abilities.

For many years batting average was seen as the standard for measuring hitting ability. Batting average was very useful because it had been around long enough that it had become easy to calculate and to understand in the context of historical records and it seemed closely related to hitting ability. It was hard for a really bad hitter to have a really good batting average. It was not a perfect measure, however, and as more questions were asked about the usefulness of batting average as a measure, it became clear that on-base percentage (OBP) was a more useful measure, using a better though still not perfect data set. Because OBP was not a historically valued statistic, teams that used it early were able to find hidden value in players. Hitting measures continue to evolve, of course, suggesting that we still do not have a precise measurement of hitting ability, but the statistics that we do have allow decision makers to have more certainty in their evaluation of the players. Numerous new metrics (see table 4.1 for some examples) in a variety of sports are helping decision makers reduce uncertainty around their evaluations of players and teams.

Another example of the value of quantifying skills and attributes is the analysis that is done around amateur drafts. Start by considering

Table 4.1 Examples of New Metrics in Baseball, Basketball, and Football

Sport	New Metric	Description
Baseball	True Average (TAv)	• Measures offensive output of a batter • Weights the various possible outcomes of a plate appearance to account for the different benefits to the team of each outcome • Scaled to look like a traditional batting average for communication purposes
	Base Running Runs (BRR)	• Calculates the value a player adds through base running • Compares both positive and negative base-running outcomes
	Spatial Aggregate Fielding Evaluation (SAFE)	• Measures a player's defensive abilities • Controls for opportunities to make plays
Basketball	Offensive/ Defensive Efficiency Rating (OER/DER)	• Reflects the points a team scores/ allows per hundred possessions • Measures the overall effectiveness of an offense or a defense, controlling for pace (possessions in a game)
	Defensive Rebound Rate (DRR)	• Indicates the ability of a player/team to rebound on the defensive end • Measured as the number of defensive rebounds collected, divided by the total defensive rebounds that were available • Controls for the number of opportunities to get a rebound
	Adjusted Plus/ Minus (+/-)	• An indicator of the overall contribution a player makes to their team • Measures the effectiveness of a team's offense and defense with and without a specific player while controlling for the level of competition faced and teammates on the floor

(continued)

Table 4.1 (Continued)

Sport	New Metric	Description
Football	Total Quarterback Rating (QBR)	• A measure of the overall contribution a quarterback makes to a game/season • Values all contributions, including running and avoiding pressure, while controlling for dropped passes and other situations beyond the QB's control
	Adjusted Line Yards	• Seeks to measure the effectiveness of a team's offensive line by crediting the line only with the yardage it is most responsible for
	Adjusted Net Yards Per Attempt (ANY/A)	• Measures the efficiency of a team's passing game by adjusting total yardage earned for TDs, sacks, and interceptions

the extreme case in which no information is known about any potential draft pick (see figure 4.2). In this scenario, the decision maker can do no better than to randomly select a player and hope for the best. Here we have minimized measurement and maximized risk. As we start to add information such as scouting reports, we reduce the risk in the decision-making process. Scouting reports are not exact and are not always correct, but they provide information that reduces the risk in making a selection on draft day. Now we add the ability to interview players before the draft. The interview process adds more information about how the player handles himself and reacts in different scenarios as well as insight into his background and personality. The interviews are an additional piece of information that further reduces the risk in selecting a player. Finally, we add the ability to analyze the quantitative information from the player's amateur performances. Here the statistical analysis of the player's skills and how those skills project to the professional level provides an additional piece of information. The analysis is not an exact measurement of how well the athlete performs in different aspects of the game, nor does it provide an exact projection of how the athlete will perform at the professional level. It does, however, provide the decision maker with more information that will further reduce the risk of making a draft pick.

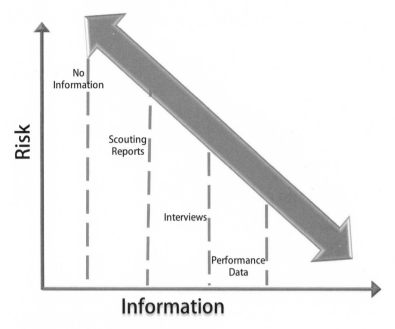

Figure 4.2 Risk vs. Information Trade-off

Leading up to the 2008 NBA draft, one of the questions that the Seattle Supersonics were dealing with was whether they should draft a center or a point guard. With the fourth pick in the draft, they were likely to have the opportunity to draft a quality player at either position, and both were positions of need for the team. As their quantitative analyst, I was asked about whether, when building a championship team, it was more important to have a top-level point guard or center. Analyzing this question from several different perspectives (playoff teams vs. total wins vs. championships and so on) I used data from twenty NBA seasons to try to deliver some insight to the choice. The multiple analyses suggested that while teams have been successful with both approaches, a top-level point guard seemed to have more long-term value than a top-level center. This analysis was one more piece of information that the Supersonics could use to help reduce the risk around their decision about which player to draft.

The quantitative information in this example plays the same role as any other information: it is one more piece in the puzzle. It helps the decision maker see a more complete picture of the athlete's future at the professional level. It is quantitative and so differs from the qualitative information provided by scouts, but it should not be viewed as an exact measurement but rather a measurement that helps put all of the other information in context and as a platform to ask questions. The process of using all of the available information to dig deeper into the athlete's potential and ask more questions actually produces even more information as the various types of information are combined and analyzed, further reducing the risk involved in the decision.

ANALYTICS AND HIRING A COACH

NFL teams do not generally use much quantitative analysis in the hiring of a head coach. The argument against the use of quantitative analysis has been that since we can point to examples of successful and unsuccessful coaches from a variety of different backgrounds, there are too many intangibles involved in what leads to head-coaching success in the NFL. This is an instance of a narrow idea of what quantitative analysis can provide. Clearly, there are successful head coaches from a variety of backgrounds. Jimmy Johnson was a successful college coach before coaching the Cowboys to two Super Bowl wins; Bill Belichick was a previously unsuccessful NFL head coach before finding success with the Patriots; Vince Lombardi was a successful offensive coordinator before winning the first two Super Bowls as the Packers head coach; and Andy Reid was a quarterbacks coach before embarking on a successful career with the Eagles. These examples suggest that there is no unique path to success as an NFL head coach.

Hiring a head coach has proven to be a risky process, and, just as with the draft, asking questions and adding new information to the process can help reduce the inherent risk. There are few decisions that have more impact on an NFL franchise than the selection of the head coach. We have seen great coaches quickly turn a team with what is perceived to be marginal talent into consistent contenders and also seen coaches fail to come anywhere near a successful season with a team that appears to have a lot of promise. Typically, the process of hiring a head coach involves assembling a pool of potential candidates based from a variety of backgrounds (currently successful assistant coaches, long-time successful college coaches, former NFL head coaches, for example) and subjecting them to a rigorous interview process to determine if they have the skills to lead the team.

One NFL franchise went through the process of hiring a head coach and made what turned out to be a poor decision. The team performed well below expectations, and ownership felt it had to move on to a different head coach. Instead of using the same process that led to the previous choice, the top decision makers at the team started to ask questions. They asked what elements of a candidate's background are most likely to produce a successful head coach. Once the decision makers started to ask these questions, the decision maker and the analysts could discuss what elements might be important: years coaching in the NFL, previous head-coaching experience at any level, previous NFL playing experience, Super Bowl wins as a coordinator, winning percentage as a college coach, etc. A long list emerged of potential pieces of the head-coaching puzzle. The analyst was then able take that list of potential elements and assemble the relevant data on potential head coaches in the NFL over the previous twenty seasons.

Before the analysis could move forward, however, the decision makers had to define and establish what it was to be a successful head coach. This required the decision makers to set the bar. Was it playoff success in multiple seasons? Is any head coach who wins the Super Bowls a successful head coach? How many division titles are required to be considered successful? Is there an element of longevity required? This questioning process allowed the decision makers to firmly establish in their minds what they were trying to find in a head coach and allowed the analyst to understand clearly what it was they were trying to measure.

The goal of the questions the NFL team raised, however, was not to find the unique path to success or to seek out some concrete guarantee that it was going to make the best hire but rather to establish what elements and experiences in a coach's background lead to a greater probability of success. The decision makers accepted from the beginning that there was going to be risk in the decision and that the quantitative analysis could help them reduce but not eliminate that risk. They used the analysis to give themselves the highest probability of success.

The result of the analysis was a grading scale that gave a score to each element of a candidate's background that was found to have a significant effect on success. This allowed the decision makers to be more fully informed about the risk they were assuming with each candidate. Candidates who scored poorly on the grading scale (such as the team's previous head coach) were riskier choices, and those that scored well carried less risk. The decision makers could see that hiring a coach who scored poorly meant accepting more risk, and so they would need to have a clear rationale as to why this particular candidate would succeed despite twenty years of data suggesting he is unlikely to. The team chose a candidate that scored high on their scale, minimizing the risk that they were taking on, and the team's results under the new head coach thus far certainly suggest that it was a successful hire.

Even with this analysis there is no guarantee that the coach the team hired would be successful. The success of the analysis was not dependent on the outcome of the hire but on the process the team went through and the front office's confidence that it made the right decision in the end. The analysis was successful because it allowed the decision makers to clarify in their own minds what they meant when they said they were looking for a successful coach, to identify candidates that had the highest probability of being successful, and to make a fully informed decision. The candidates identified still went through a rigorous interview process so that the decision makers had as much information as possible to reduce risk as much as they could.

FIVE QUESTIONS FOR ALL ANALYSES

The purpose of exploring how analysis can be used is to demonstrate the need for decision makers to ask good questions and to show that they can only do that when they understand what they can expect from analysis. Any time a decision maker is faced with a difficult, risky decision, analysis can help inform and reduce the risk around the decision provided the right questions are asked, particularly questions that have not been quantified before. Analysis will never eliminate the risk in a decision, but it can reduce it.

Once an analyst delivers the answers, the decision maker must evaluate how useful the result is and how much the uncertainty that was previously in the decision is reduced by the information presented in the analysis. Once a number is served to a decision maker, the tendency is to treat that number as a fact and either accept it as truth or dismiss it as trivial. In most cases the proper way to understand the analysis lies somewhere in between these two extremes. Only the decision maker can truly decide how to weight the results of quantitative analysis. But by probing the result and the process that led to the result with five basic questions, the decision maker can start to understand how much confidence the analysis deserves:

1. What was the thought process that led to the analysis?
2. What is the context of the result?
3. How much uncertainty is in the analysis?
4. How does the result inform the decision-making process?
5. How can we further reduce the uncertainty?

These questions may lead to further analysis or increased confidence in the result or might point to areas in which gathering more data in the future might be extremely valuable. It is always important that the decision maker treat this as an ongoing process and that, just because some analysis may not be as complete as everyone would like at the time a decision must be made, the process should continue as similar decisions are likely to present themselves in the future.

What Was the Thought Process That Led to the Analysis?

EXPLAIN MY VIEW OF THE ISSUE

Beginning with this question allows the decision maker to have confidence that the analyst is viewing the issue from a similar point of view as the decision maker, which is vital. If the analysis is not built to answer the right question, then it will most likely produce the wrong answer. So this question draws the analysts out and forces them to explain their view of the issue.

For example, a decision maker in basketball may ask the analytics team how good an offensive rebounder a particular player is. The analysts have the motion-capture data along with traditional play-by-play data. There are multiple angles that the analysts could take to try to answer the question. They could just calculate the percentage of missed shots on the offensive end that the player is on the floor for and rebounds, they could estimate the probability that a player would get a rebound based on the player's distance from the rim at the time of the shot, estimate the probability that a player would get a rebound based on the number of defensive players between himself and the rim at the time of the shot, or track the player's reaction and movement toward the hoop from the time the shot is taken to the time the ball hits the rim. These are not the only possibilities, but how the analysts approach this basic question gives the decision maker insight into what the analysts are trying to do, and the analysts' view of the game in general. As the analysts explain how they are approaching the question, the decision maker can make suggestions on dimensions of the issue that the analysts have not considered (e.g., how many of those offensive rebounds are off the player's own missed shots?).

For the sake of efficient use of time, it is best to ask this question at the beginning of any specific project. This ensures that the analysts are headed in the right direction before they actually design their analysis and choose their methods. However, it is important that it be asked at some point so that anyone using the completed analysis understands what questions it was really answering.

What Is the Context of the Result?

Every analysis needs to be viewed within the proper context, or it will risk being interpreted incorrectly. Not investigating the context of the analysis will lead to, at best, a naïve interpretation of the result and maybe a missed opportunity to understand how valuable a result can be. This is true for all types of information, not just quantitative analysis, as every decision maker in sports can attest. When decision makers in sports watch game film, they see what unfolds in front of them in a more nuanced manner than a typical fan—they see the entire context. For example, in football, if a defensive end bursts off the line and runs unblocked into the backfield and sacks the quarterback, the immediate reaction of the fan or untrained viewer is that the offensive lineman lined up in front of the defensive end and who appeared to move out of the way of the rush was to blame for the sack. The trained observer may notice that the offensive lineman was actually moving within a blocking scheme and had a different responsibility on the play while a running back had mistakenly left the backfield to run a route instead of staying in to block.

This level of context and sophistication has to be brought to the use of analysis as well. To continue the football example, an analyst may be asked to evaluate the pass-blocking ability of a particular left tackle from a different team. The analyst and decision maker have a conversation about the thought process that the analyst will use to build the analysis, and the analyst comes back with a report that explains the left tackle gives up a sack on approximately one of every one hundred pass plays. The naïve use of this result is for the decision maker to compare that analysis to his left tackle, who gives up a sack on one of every fifty pass plays. This direct comparison strongly favors the external left tackle, who appears to give up sacks at half the rate of the player on the roster. Now is when context is crucial. It may turn out, for example that the analyst incorporated a quarterback's time to throw into the analysis and that the sack rate presented actually represents how well the left tackle blocks when the quarterback throws the ball in 2.5 seconds. If the quarterback for the decision maker's team has an average time to throw of 3.2 seconds, then the two sack rates are not comparable, and the initial analysis may in fact be misleading. Armed with the context of the result, however, the decision maker can now push deeper, asking about comparable numbers for their own players to make honest comparisons.

How Much Uncertainty Is in the Analysis?

There are two types of uncertainty that need to be clearly identified and understood in any analysis: variability in the result and the effects of variables not included in the analysis. Every time we measure a player's skills or their impact on a team, the specific number reported is a best estimate, but the level of accuracy of that estimate is dependent upon both the data available to the analysis (sample size) and the methods used to make the estimate. More data (increased sample size) lead to results with less variability, and more sophisticated analysis can lead to more accurate results (as the analysis includes more information) but may also increase the variability around the result. We can measure this variability in the estimate and use it in the decision-making process to assess how much the analysis has reduced the uncertainty around the decision. Variables may not be included in an analysis for a variety of reasons, and their full impact cannot be known. The missing variables should be identified, however, so the decision maker knows what is not included in the analysis, offering a deeper understanding of the areas of uncertainty that remain in the decision-making process.

The issue of variability in a result is fairly intuitive: when we have more data we can be more certain about the result. This is true in all research, and in quantitative analysis, we can quantify the variability.

For example, if a decision maker in football wants to know how many yards per carry an upcoming opponent gains when two different running backs carry the ball, the analyst is probably faced with two different samples. The analyst can pull the data and may find that the result is the same for both backs; whichever back carries the ball, the team averages 3.4 yards per carry. If one of the backs has carried the ball fifty times so far that season and the other ten, there is a lot more variability in the reported average for the back with fewer carries. That variability can be measured, and figure 4.3 represents this comparison graphically. The range of likely outcomes depicted in the figure represents the range in which there is a 95 percent probability of the "true value." In this analysis, we cannot with 100 percent certainty know how the opposing offense will perform with either back, but we can, within the context of our analysis, define the range in which there is a very high probability that the actual performance will fall.

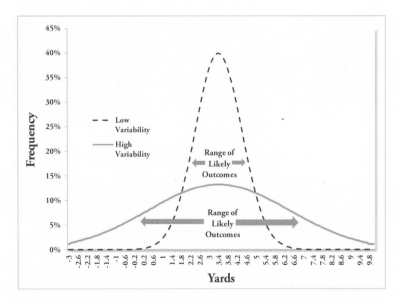

Figure 4.3 Comparison of Variability for Two Backs with the Same Carry Average

The range of likely outcomes, or, in this case, performance of the opposing offense, is a lot higher for the back with fewer carries. For the back with fewer carries, the analysis suggests that the most likely outcome is 3.4 yards per carry, and that we are 95 percent sure that the offense will register between −0.2 and 7 yards per carry with this back. For the higher-carry back, the analysis suggests that the most likely outcome is also 3.4 yards per carry and that we are 95 percent sure that the offense will register between 1.8 and 5 yards per carry.

The inclusion of the variability in the analysis is important for a variety of reasons. For example, in the case demonstrated in figure 4.3, if the team holds its opponent to 1.5 yards per carry, then it has performed exceedingly well if the low-variability back was carrying the ball, but it has not outperformed expectations if the high-variability back was carrying the ball.

How Does the Result Inform the Decision-Making Process?

Once the result and its variability are fully understood, the decision maker must consider how the result fits into the larger context of the decision. This starts with understanding how the analysis is consistent with other types of information pertaining to the decision, how it is contradictory, and where it is silent. This step of placing the analysis in the context of all of the other information at the decision maker's disposal identifies the areas in which more information is needed and often points toward the way to find it.

Consider the case of an NFL general manager trying to decide whether to sign a free-agent defensive lineman to serve as the team's primary pass-rushing specialist. The previous season the player posted an impressive sack total against generally well regarded opponents. The scouts watched him work in person and on film and felt that he had the speed and agility to be a very strong if not dominant pass rusher on a consistent basis; they also had talked to a variety people that knew him personally and gained the impression that he was a natural leader—a good locker-room guy. The team's analyst examined the player's results from the predraft combine as well as the play-by-play data from each of the player's three NFL seasons. The analyst's conclusions were that while the player possessed the athleticism to play the position at a high level, the player was unlikely to continue to pressure or sack opposing quarterbacks at the level of the previous season.

The general manager is now tasked with examining all the information before him and making a decision with inherent risk. Clearly, the scouts and analyst agree on the player's athletic abilities; both saw him as a high-level performer. There was a clear disagreement on the future production of the player, however, as the scouts felt that the previous season showed that the athlete's abilities would lead to consistent high-level performance. The analysis was silent on the player's leadership qualities and the effect that they would have on the team.

The general manager's perception was that the source of the conflicting information was the player's high sack total from the previous season, so he tasked both the scouts and the analyst to go back to those plays to better understand whether they were evidence of future dominance or some sort of aberration that would not reoccur. Once the scouts and analyst examined those plays more closely, it became clear that on the majority of those plays, the QB had held the ball much longer than average, which created an easier sack opportunity for the lineman. This analysis suggested that the high sack total was not representative of the player's true skill, so no offer was made.

How Can We Further Reduce the Uncertainty Around the Decision?

The question about further reducing uncertainty is normally focused on the analysis, but often a more thorough vetting of the decision is more valuable. With the result of the analysis and its effect on the decision known, revisiting the core decision allows the decision maker and analyst to view the decision with reduced uncertainty and reevaluate next steps. This line of questioning highlights the cyclical nature of the analytic process, in which there is always another, deeper layer that can be analyzed to the benefit of the decision maker.

A general manager in the NBA, for example, was in the position of deciding between two young shooting guards (Players A and B) that were both well liked by the scouting staff and both available for the same trade package. Both players had been in the league for two seasons. Player A was a top-ten pick in the draft, twenty-three years old, and a starter for a nonplayoff team for two seasons. Player B was a late first-round pick, twenty-four years old, and a backup on a playoff contender behind an all-star shooting guard. The general manager asked an analyst to project both players' performance over the next three seasons to see which one was more likely to develop into a high-level starter. After analyzing the data, the analyst reported back that while both players projected to be high-level players in the near future, there was less variation in Player A's projections, suggesting that there was less uncertainty about Player A's future than Player B's future.

Working through the analysis, the analyst explained the thought process that lead to the analysis (i.e., future projections based on the performance data for each player, compared to previous players of the same age and playing the same total minutes). The analyst then provided the context for the results, making sure to explain how the performance data for each player were adjusted for the system that he played in and the role that he fulfilled (starter vs. sixth man, primary scorer vs. facilitator, and so on). The analyst then explained that the main source of increased uncertainty for Player B was the expanded minutes played that Player B would be expected to take on as a starter, which led to a wider range of future performance than for Player A. Finally, the analyst suggested that the analysis in general agreed with the scouts, that both players were likely to be perform as high-level starters over the next two seasons, but that there was less risk in adding Player A than Player B.

The general manager took in the analysis and began to ask questions centered around both players' shooting ability. Player B had a higher shooting percentage than Player A, and since the general manager was most concerned with adding a high-level shooter to the roster, he was not convinced that Player A was the best choice and asked the analyst to delve deeper into each players' shooting ability to further reduce the uncertainty around the decision. The analyst looked at both players' shooting data and started to adjust their shooting percentages for different locations on the court.[3] This process led the analyst to separate each players' shooting skills into pure shooting skill (i.e., the ability to make shots, adjusting for distance) and the ability to select high-value shots.[4] The differentiation between shot-making ability and shot-selection ability led the analyst to find that despite Player B's higher shooting percentage, Player A had better shot-making and shot-selection abilities. Player B's higher shooting percentage came from a higher number of midrange jump shots. Player A took more three-point shots, so his shooting percentage was lower, but scored more points per shot than Player B, whose midrange two-point shots were made more often but for fewer points. The detailed shooting analysis further reduced the uncertainty for the general manager around the choice between the two players.

ANALYSIS AS PROCESS

These five questions provide a process for decision makers' incorporation of high-level statistical results into the decision-making process. The overall goal, from a process perspective, is to treat the analysis, first, as part of the decision-making process and, second, as an ongoing process. Incorporating statistical analysis allows the decision maker to have the large amounts of raw quantitative data turned into usable information that can augment other types of information. This is most effective when decision makers view the analysis as a tool that reduces uncertainty, can help confirm other information, or, in instances in which it is contradictory, can lead to more and deeper questions about the analysis and the decisions that are being made. Viewing the analysis as an ongoing process ensures that the analysis is always questioned, refined, and understood more fully. Establishing these processes will give the organization a better chance at maximizing their analytic investment.

ADDITIONAL RESOURCES

The following resources provide more technical information on the tools of statistical analysis and their application to sports:

Albert, Jim. *Teaching Statistics Using Baseball* (Washington, D.C.: The Mathematical Association of America, 2003).

Carroll, Bob, Pete Palmer, and John Thorn. *The Hidden Game of Football* (New York: Grand Central, 1988).

Hubbard, Douglas W. *How to Measure Anything: Finding the Value of Intangibles in Business* (Hoboken, N.J.: Wiley, 2010).

Journal of Quantitative Analysis in Sports (published quarterly by De Gruyter).

Oliver, Dean. *Basketball on Paper: Rules and Tools for Performance Analysis* (Dulles, Va.: Brassey, 2004).

Tango, Tom M., Mitchel G. Lichtman, and Andrew E. Dolphin. *The Book: Playing the Percentages in Baseball* (Washington, D.C.: Potomac, 2007).

5

NEW METRICS

"What gets measured gets managed."
—PETER DRUCKER, AUTHOR AND MANAGEMENT CONSULTANT

There has been significant attention paid over the last ten years, both in sports and in business, to the creation of new metrics. Decision makers have been using new metrics to gauge everything from team ability to brand image. As data become more accessible, decision makers have found clearer insight into their organizations and the nature of the decisions they face through the use of metrics that did not exist even a few years ago. One of the key roles of the analyst is to create these new and meaningful metrics.

New metrics provide decision makers with new kinds of information regarding the performance, progress, and potential of players and teams. Metrics also save time because they summarize data and provide insight that might have previously been available only by sorting through raw data. In order to create a valuable new metric, the goal (both what is being measured and how the metric will be used) needs to be clearly established. In addition to the goals for the metric, the analyst should consider how to design and present the metric to allow it to be efficiently incorporated into the decision-making process. The establishment of a new metric can be thought of as a four-phase process: opportunity, survey, analysis, and communication (figure 5.1).

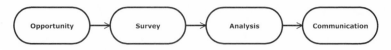

Figure 5.1 The Four Phases of Metric Creation

A successful metric provides new or more accurate information for the decision-making process. The four-phase process increases the odds that the end product will be as informative and useful as possible. While most successful metrics are held privately by the teams that developed them, some have been created publicly and can be used as examples to illustrate the process. One generally successful public metric is John Hollinger's Player Efficiency Rating (PER). This metric is cited regularly in articles in *Sports Illustrated* and on ESPN, calculated on most basketball analytic websites, and mentioned, at least, in many NBA front offices. Tracking the creation of PER through the four-phase process helps identify the source of its success as well as areas in which a more careful process might have led to even better results.

OPPORTUNITY

During the opportunity phase, the need for a new metric or for improvements on current metrics is identified. The process usually begins with a series of questions. A new metric might be needed to establish the effect that player X's leadership has on his team's performance or whether player Y really makes her teammates better. An existing metric might need to be refined to establish how playing with an elite quarterback affects a running back's average yards per carry or how the type of shot faced affects a goalie's save percentage. These lead to more questions regarding what is known and what is not known, and eventually the concept for a new metric is born. The goal of this phase is a definition of the purpose of the metric and a sense of how it will ideally fit into the decision-making process.

For Hollinger, one the driving questions was how to know whether an NBA player was better than his backup. In order to see whether one player actually benefits his team more than another, all of the ways a player might contribute need to be considered. Hollinger saw that there was no clear way to compare the contributions of an excellent perimeter shooter with a high-level rebounder. The opportunity for a new and useful metric was clear, and the need that emerged was for a tool or set of tools that allowed for fair comparisons of players.

SURVEY

The survey phase identifies and examines the state of both the relevant statistics currently in use and the availability of relevant data. Typically, whatever the goal of the new metric, there will have been previous attempts at filling the need. These previous attempts may not have managed to capture all of the important dimensions of the need or might have been scouting-based subjective grades or qualitative analysis. It is important to identify previous attempts to answer the same question in order to clarify the goal of the new metric. Identifying them will also inform the decision-making context to be used in the analysis. The result of the survey phase should be a clear and realistic concept for how to build a metric that will help inform the decision-making process.

The survey phase for the creation of PER began with identifying the tools currently used to gauge the effect players have on their team's success. These included statistics such as points per game, rebounds per game, and field-goal percentage. The comparison of players was done typically by comparing this array of statistics, but Hollinger identified two key issues: the statistics were not comparable across players, and the statistics were not comparable to one another.

The existing basketball statistics did not take into account differences in playing time, which rendered them generally not comparable across players because a player's opportunity to create points, rebounds, or turnovers is controlled by time on the court. A player who averages ten minutes a game has fewer opportunities to score than a player who plays thirty minutes a game. A starter may have a higher points-scored per game average than a better-shooting backup because he is on the court three times as much.

The statistics were not comparable to one another because they measured different outcomes; there is no clear manner to compare the value of a defensive rebound with two points scored or a personal foul. For example, during the 2011–12 NBA season, center DeJuan Blair of the San Antonio Spurs averaged 9.5 points, 5.5 rebounds, and 1.2 assists per game while shooting 53.4 percent from the field, and Spurs center Tiago Splitter averaged 9.3 points, 5.2 rebounds, and 1.1 assists per game while shooting 61.8 percent from the field (see table 5.1). Based on these statistics, Blair had a slight edge in points, rebounds, and assists, and Splitter converted a higher percentage of his shots. Are the small advantages in the first three categories enough to suggest that Blair is the better player, or is Splitter's superior FG% the controlling factor? As Hollinger was trying to decide between two players, it became clear that a more systematic approach that allowed for the comparison across both players and statistics would create a clearer picture of the player's overall contribution.

With these clarifications in mind, Hollinger could gather the relevant data. As the purpose of the metric was to combine all contributions into one metric, all of the measured court activities should enter into the calculation. Classifying the available data into the type of contribution (positive or negative) allows for the beginning of a framework for the new metric (see figure 5.2). A clear understanding of each traditional statistic pointed toward how all the pieces might be combined. The process of classifying the data can lead to an insight such as listing field-goal attempts as a negative contribution. This insight

Table 5.1 Averages per Game for the 2011–12 NBA Season

Player	Points	Rebounds	Assists	FG%
DeJuan Blair	9.5	5.5	1.2	53.4
Tiago Splitter	9.3	5.2	1.1	61.8

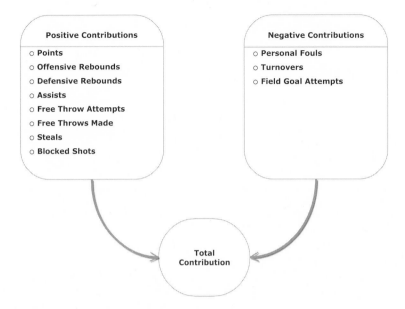

Figure 5.2 Metric-Creation Model

came from thinking about two players who were exactly the same in every category except that one had more field goal attempts than the other. The player with the higher field-goal attempts but same number of points scored uses more resources (shots) to create the same output (points), which means that the player with fewer field-goal attempts is, in a sense, more efficient. That insight then grew into the key concept of PER—comparing players not on their gross contributions (points per game) but on how efficiently they produce. A measure of efficiency across the traditional statistics allows players to be compared to one another directly, which tells decision makers how effectively two different players contribute to the team.

ANALYSIS

In the analysis phase the new metric is actually built and tested. The statistical tools and mathematical reasoning of the analyst are now applied to the data to create a metric that fills the previously identified need. Part of the analysis phase may also be identifying data that have not been previously collected but could add significant value to the decision-making process. The analyst can investigate the feasibility of collecting the data as well as potential methods for working around missing data.

Clearly defining the goal of the metric is important in this phase both for the actual creation of the metric and also in evaluating whether the metric does what is needed. For example, metrics can be descriptive or predictive. The goal of a descriptive metric is to tell the story of what has occurred, and the goal of a predictive statistic is to be an indicator of the future. Understanding this distinction in the analysis phase allows the analyst to test the statistic for the necessary properties.

During the analysis phase, the analyst needs to document the process, recording how she created the metric and the evidence she has that the metric serves the stated purpose. This documentation provides justification for whether to use the metric in the decision-making process, assists other analytic personnel in incorporating the metric into their work, and details the analyst's process so that it can be reviewed either for improvement in the metric or evaluation of the analyst's work. Once the metric has been tested, the analyst is confident that it measures what is needed, and all documentation is completed, the analyst can move to the communication stage.

In what can be viewed as his analysis phase, Hollinger worked through the math to understand the relative effect of points vs. rebounds vs. fouls. This resulted in a complex formula that included team and individual factors and corrected for issues such as minutes played and the pace of play to get to a measure of total efficiency. The measure converted all contributions (positive and negative) into a consistent measure of effectiveness and put them within an efficiency framework based on possessions played instead of games played. As he worked he identified important missing data, such as the number of missed shots (for either team) that happened while the player was on the court. Each missed shot is an opportunity for a rebound, so knowing the number of opportunities a player had provides important context for the total rebounds that the player actually got. While this data was not readily available when PER was first created, Hollinger was able to create a reasonable estimate of the missing data to incorporate in the new metric.

Creating, testing, and documenting the new metric came as a natural outgrowth of Hollinger's role as a sportswriter. He thoroughly vetted PER with a wide audience by testing the metric against current players, constructing arguments when PER differed from common wisdom about a player, and repeatedly describing the basis for the metric. For example, Hollinger, fans, and decision makers with NBA teams can now use PER to compare DeJuan Blair's total contribution with Tiago Splitter's on the basis of total efficiency. For the 2011–12 season, Blair's PER was 17.6, and Splitter's was 20.5. Clearly, Splitter's performance was more efficient (he had the higher PER), but to fully understand the meaning of this difference (i.e., is 2.9 a big or small difference in PER?), we must move to the communication phase.

COMMUNICATION

During the communication phase the analyst must consider how to provide the proper evidence and context for the new metric in order to demonstrate its value to the decision makers. Decision makers need to clearly understand the skill or event the metric is measuring, how the metric differs from previous measurements, and why they should use it. Additionally, they must be able to easily interpret the metric. One of the reasons decision makers continue to use older metrics is that they understand how to interpret them. Batting average in baseball is one example of this. Decision makers in baseball were brought up on batting average and so instinctively feel they know what it means and what are good and bad batting averages. They have a feel for how much better a .350 hitter is than a .275 hitter.

They have a context of the numbers. So while batting average is now generally acknowledged to be a subpar measure of a player's offensive skill as it does not include the outcomes of all plate appearances (such as walks), its use persists because decision makers are comfortable with it as a measure.

When presenting a new metric that decision makers have no familiarity with, the analyst needs to think about both the scale that the metric uses and its context. The issue of scale is important because without some understanding of what is a good number and what is a bad number, the decision maker would have to continually check the metric' documentation to reference relative values. Some scales, such as a percentiles, are more easily and widely understood. Reporting the results of the new metric on a percentile scale allows decision makers to immediately engage with the metric because most decision makers are familiar with the concept that being in the 75th percentile is much better than being in the 55th percentile. The percentile scale is not always the right way to report a metric (reporting in terms of wins created or points created can also be useful, for example), but however the metric is reported, attention to the scale is a key component of whether the metric is adopted into the decision-making process.

The scale helps provide context for the numbers being reported, but equally important is the context of those numbers. The context is the set of players, teams, events, and so on that are being compared. Are all players in the league being compared, just those of a particular age, or just those of a particular position? Is the metric adjusted for the level of the competition? Whether the event was on the road or at home? These are just some of the dimensions that can affect how a metric is viewed. Context can have major effect on the information derived from the metric. If, for example, an MLB player is reported to have an on-base percentage in the 50th percentile when compared to all MLB players, that suggests that he is an average hitter. But if we know that the player is a pitcher and that he ranks in the 80th percentile in OBP among pitchers, that paints a different picture of the player's potential to add value to the team.

The communication phase is perhaps where PER could be improved. While Hollinger is a good writer and repeatedly explains the measure well in his articles, there is nothing natural about the scale that PER is reported on, so the user of the information may need to find the proper frame of reference before the values can be understood. Returning to the previous comparison of Splitter and Blair, PER tells us that Splitter's total contribution (20.5) was more efficient than Blair's (17.6), but unless a decision maker has spent extensive time previously working with PER it is unlikely that he would be comfortable interpreting whether this is a large or small difference or whether either player is above or below average according to the metric. PER was built to have a score of 15 indicate an average season. Locking the average value for a season is helpful as it allows for more accurate comparison of value across seasons, but the rating of 15 does not relate directly to points scored, wins created, percentiles, or any other scale that a decision maker understands from previous experience. Given this general lack of familiarity with the metric, it becomes harder to se in the decision-making process.

Knowing that an average season is pinned to a rating of 15 allows the decision maker to see that both Splitter and Blair had above-average efficiency. But still lacking is an idea of how much above average each player is; there is no context for their peers beyond the average player. To apply the proper context to the values, consider one of Hollinger's motivating questions from the opportunity phase: should a starter be replaced by his backup? This question suggests a direct comparison between two players at the same position on the same team. Splitter and Blair provide just such a comparison, so using position as context for the statistic can be illuminating. Figure 5.3 shows the distributions of PER for centers and guards who played at least 1,500 minutes from the 2007–8 to 2011–12 seasons. The distribution of PER differs greatly for the two positions. For centers, 78 percent had a PER between 14.2 and 19.6 (the average center had a PER of 17). Only 64 percent of guards had a PER in the same range (the average guard had a PER of 15). These differences suggest that overall PER was higher for centers and that the values were not as

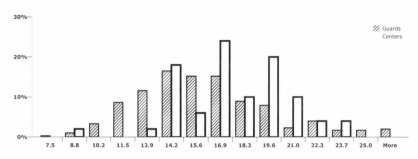

Figure 5.3 Distribution of PER for Centers and Guards
Min. 1,500 minutes played, 2007–8 through 2011–12 seasons.

spread out—centers as a group had relatively smaller differences in PER than guards.

Using the centers as context for the Splitter/Blair comparison, the PER values can be translated into percentiles so that Splitter's efficiency is in the 88th percentile and Blair's is in the 58th percentile. Using this context, the decision maker can see that Splitter's performance is nearing elite levels while Blair's is just slightly above average. A decision maker can now use this information more confidently in deciding which player should get more minutes. The difference between their performances is clearly quite large when it is placed in the proper context.

Using their position as context situates Splitter and Blair's PER scores and informs deciding which player should play more for the team. If the question changes, however, the context may change as well. Consider now a decision maker contemplating which player to sign to a long-term contract. The question changes from current performance to future performance. With the change in focus, the context of the evaluation needs to change as well. One factor in long-term contracts is whether a player has the potential to improve. While it is certainly possible for an analyst to do a long-term projection for each player based on PER and other statistics, it can be useful to simply put these player's performance in the context of other similar players. Splitter was twenty-seven during the 2011–12 season, and Blair was twenty-two. Given Blair's youth, his lower PER seems reasonable, and perhaps, from a long-term perspective, he has the potential to surpass Splitter. Splitter's performance was in the 84th percentile for twenty-seven-year-old centers playing 1,500 or more minutes, and Blair's performance was in the 76th percentile for twenty-two-year-old centers playing 1,500 or more minutes. Given the context of age, the two performances seem much closer together, and a decision regarding the long-term prospects of both players is certainly less clear than the immediate decision regarding current playing time.

The comparison of Splitter and Blair through PER is useful because it highlights the need to create metrics that can be readily understood and used in the decision-making process. Once a metric is on an easily understandable scale, decision makers will naturally have more confidence in it because they have more a more intuitive grasp of what it means. Once the purpose of the metric is understood, then the proper context can be established for it. The four-phase approach to building metrics increases the chances that a metric will be successful because it reinforces these key principles.

PASSING METRICS

As discussed earlier, the process of creating new metrics often begins through a series of questions. Before the 2008 NBA draft, questions arose around Russell Westbrook, an extremely athletic guard who had played two seasons at UCLA, predominantly as a shooting guard, not a point guard. The Seattle Supersonics were in need of a point guard, not a shooting guard, but all members of the personnel department loved the athleticism, work ethic, and defensive abilities of Westbrook. As the team's analyst, I found that Westbrook's performance data suggested a high probability of success in the NBA. I analyzed his performance using my model for shooting guards and my model for point guards, and both agreed. The problem, however, was that since Westbrook had played primarily shooting guard, it was not statistically valid to compare his performance data with the performance data of other point guards, and since the team wanted him to play point guard, it was not very useful to project him as a shooting guard.

There were significant discussions among the personnel staff as to whether Westbrook's array of skills would translate into effective point-guard play in the NBA. A point guard is the leader of the offense and is charged with distributing the ball to his teammates, so our questions centered around his ability to effectively pass the ball. More specifically, could Westbrook make the right decisions and distribute the ball effectively so that the team's offense could function at a high level. This was the opportunity phase for creating a new metric because new information was needed to help reduce the uncertainty around the decision whether to draft Westbrook. The specific opportunity was to create a metric that measured Westbrook's ability to effectively pass the ball.

With the opportunity identified, I entered the survey phase and began to look at the existing metrics used to assess a player's passing ability. The most basic passing metric is the assist. An assist is recorded for a player when he makes a pass to a teammate that results in a shot being taken and made. Traditionally, a player's assists are counted either in total or on a per-game or per-minute basis, and players with high assist numbers are thought to be good passers. The more advanced version is assist percentage, which estimates the percentage of a team's made shots a given player assisted. However, these measures of passing ability were flawed in Westbrook's case for two reasons. The first is a general data-collection problem in that an assist, unlike the result of a shot, is an inherently subjective statistic. There is no precise, universally applied definition of an assist, and it is fairly easy for a scorekeeper to award assists that are undeserved or not award an assist that is deserved.[1] Additionally, assists, no matter how they are defined, are only recorded when a shot is made, therefore, players on poor shooting teams may make a lot of good passes that never get recognized as assists because their teammates miss the shots. The second issue, which is specific to Westbrook, is that his role on the UCLA team did not put him in a position to make passes that lead to assists as frequently as a traditional point guard, so his assist numbers cannot be fairly compared to those of a traditional point guard. Westbrook's traditional and even advanced assist statistics were not necessarily representative of his passing ability. The survey of passing metrics led to the conclusion that a new metric was needed that accurately and consistently measured a player's passing abilities.

The results of the survey phase suggested a need for metric that looked at a player's specific passes and their effect on the team's offense. The hypothesis that I settled on for building the metric is that a player's passing ability, at least in part, can be measured by the change in the team's shooting percentage when the player passes the ball to the shooter. The idea was to compare the team's shooting percentage on unassisted shots to the team's shooting percentage on shots in which Westbrook made the pass to the shooter, and also to shots when other teammates made the pass to the shooter (adjusting for the distance of the shot). As no data existed on this, the only way to create the metric was to collect new data through watching film. We collected data on a variety of players, including other guards that were in the 2008 draft and NBA-level point guards in order to compare the most relevant players. Once the data were collected, I estimated the change in the probability of a shot being made if Westbrook made the pass that led to the shot. Westbrook's estimated effect on shooting percentage was better than that of UCLA point guard Darren Collison (who would become the twenty-first pick in the 2009 draft) and only slightly below that of Derrick Rose (the top pick in the 2008 draft). His effect on shooting was also comparable to many of the top point guards in the NBA, such as Jason Kidd and Steve Nash. The analysis phase thus resulted in a metric that, while certainly not the ultimate measure of passing ability, corrected many of the issues with previous passing metrics and provided some new insight into the decision that had to be made.

Entering the communication phase, the challenge was to present the new metric in an effective way and allow the decision makers to have enough confidence in the analysis to incorporate it into the decision-making process. The comparison of Westbrook's performance with those of Rose and Collison was instructive as Rose was clearly a top-level point guard so would be expected to perform well in a passing metric. Collison was the point guard on Westbrook's team and also thought to be an NBA prospect. Seeing that Collison scored well on the metric, though not as well as Westbrook, helped provide more evidence that there was some value to the metric. Finally, demonstrating that known top NBA point guards scored well on the metric and lesser point guards did not added to the evidence that it was accurate. This analysis was only one piece of information available to the decision makers for the Sonics, but it helped reduce the uncertainty around drafting Westbrook, who would go on to become an all-star point guard in his third NBA season.

6

INFORMATION SYSTEMS

Any sufficiently advanced technology is indistinguishable from magic.
—ARTHUR C. CLARKE, AUTHOR

There are two main goals of an analytics program: provide new, actionable information and save time for decision makers. Neither of these is attainable in an ongoing way without a high-quality information system. The information system is the tool that allows decision makers to access the information and analyses that will help them gain a competitive advantage. As discussed previously, teams have mountains of data. Analysts can produce high-quality, useful analysis from those data, but that investment in time and money will be wasted if a decision maker cannot access the information efficiently. Thoughtful design of these systems is vital to truly maximizing the return on the analytic investment.

When constructing an information system, there are several key, overlapping components that must be considered. In order to build an effective information system, an organization must understand its current systems, the sources of its information, how each type of information is used in the decision-making process, and how decision makers interact with the information. A clear picture of the decision-making processes is needed so that the information system will be designed specifically to support or improve the process, not hinder it. An efficient information system can save the decision makers time and ensure that they are receiving the best and most useful information. If the system does not fit into the decision makers' process however, it will not be used, and many of the potential benefits of analytics will be lost.

Teams' existing technology and personnel are often resources that can be leveraged in the creation of a more efficient information system. The Orlando Magic, for example, when building its analytics program, began by using some of the analytics personnel from the business side of the organization. This allowed the team to efficiently assess whether the technology in place on the business side could be adapted to the needs of the basketball side.

INFORMATION SYSTEMS: THE MAGNET BOARD

Every team uses information systems; those systems take many forms and are typically highly inefficient, costing decision makers time and often limiting the visibility of key information. A classic example of an information system used across sports is the magnet board. Magnet boards are metallic planes holding magnets that represents each player on the team, in the league, or in an upcoming draft class. Each player's magnet might contain some basic information, such as his or her position, team, contract status, college, age, and so on, but the amount of information on the magnet is severely constrained by its size. The magnet board can be used in a variety of ways, but it is essentially a mechanism for grouping players. The grouping may be by team, position, draft ranking, or some other factor or combination of factors. Teams can use the magnet boards in a variety of ways, including quickly viewing depth at particular positions for their competitors or grouping players in potential trades. Setting up (fifteen to twenty hours) and maintaining (one to two hours per week) a magnet board is an arduous process that is typically relegated to interns and others lower down in the organization.

The magnet board is an iconic part of the offices of professional sports teams and provides easy access to a particular set of information. It is also static. The magnet board only changes the type of information it displays when someone is tasked with changing it, and it only reflects current information when it has been manually updated. Finally, the magnet board does not allow the consumers of the information, the decision makers, to delve more deeply into any of the information that it displays. In short, the magnet board is severely limited in its usefulness, beyond providing meeting attendees something to stare at and manipulate.

Typically, when a decision maker is examining the magnet board and has an idea, she has no way of exploring that idea without turning to her computer to start pulling up applications and websites or asking other members of the team to gather answers to the questions that the idea generates. This is an incredibly inefficient process that adds significant time to the decision-making process. Instead of moving directly from idea to exploration and analysis, the decision maker has to start gathering information. This is time consuming, and it also limits the information that the decision maker can access to what she thinks she needs in that moment. The rest of the organization's information resources are not brought to bear on the idea.

An additional issue related to the magnet board is privacy. When the front office begins ranking players for its "draft board" or coaching staffs establish initial depth charts, for example, those boards are not something that the decision makers want seen by office visitors or even lower-level members of the team. The information can be highly sensitive, and decision makers do not want the media, their players, or other teams having a window into their thinking. To solve this problem, teams use a variety of mechanisms, including putting up curtains, keeping conference rooms locked, and building cabinets around the magnet boards so that no unauthorized person can see what is on them. Even with all of the attention paid to the sensitivity of the information, as long as the magnet board is set up, it is difficult to fully limit access to the information.

The other end of the spectrum from the magnet board is a fully automated system that displays (perhaps on a large screen in the meeting room) all of the information that the magnet board contains, as well as all of the other information that a decision maker might want to use. A high-quality information system that is designed to replace the magnet board and become the primary source of information for all decision makers in the office provides instant access to the most updated information in all of the team's databases.

One example of this is the Interactive, Collaborative, and Evaluation (ICE) system that has been developed by Stats LLC and has been used by the New Orleans Saints, Minnesota Timberwolves, Toronto Raptors, and Milwaukee Bucks. This system ideally replaces the magnet board and solves many of its shortcomings as an information system. The ICE system is built on top of a properly organized data system, as discussed in chapter 2, so that it can efficiently retrieve the information needed as questions are asked. It is updated in real time, not when someone has a moment. Additionally, access to the system can be easily limited to improve the security of the information. Systems such as ICE can improve the decision-making process. In particular, there is a growing demand to access information off-site and on different types of devices. The ability to have mobile access to the team's information has allowed decision makers to access information and data sources that they trust while on the road and even at games.

INFORMATION SETS

An information system can reduce the time a decision maker spends gathering information by enabling access to all relevant information through a single application. In order to create that access, however, a complete understanding of the kinds information used in the decision-making process is vital.

Some information is easily identified as part of the decision-making process. Salary data, for example is vital when making decisions around the salary cap. Other information may not be as obvious. When considering the set of information needed to evaluate a player, a decision maker may use scouting reports, medical reports, and performance metrics but may not necessarily think of team needs or input from a coach as part of the information set. Identifying the less

Figure 6.1 Player-Related Information

obvious pieces of information that relate to a decision is vital so that all of the information is presented in a cohesive fashion and in the proper context (see figure 6.1).

Personnel executives understand the strengths and weaknesses of their team. They may not, however, always have all of those strengths and weaknesses in mind when evaluating a player. Once the needs of the team are integrated into the information presented about a player, the decision maker can see all of the needs a player fills rather than the narrower set he was focused on when he began his analysis. Defining information sets makes sure all of the necessary information is presented efficiently and within the proper context so that decision makers can see all of the dimensions of an issue before taking action.

Information Levels

When formulating a plan for presenting the necessary information, decision makers and analysts need to consider when each element of each set of information is needed. Once the relevant information is gathered (figure 6.1), it must be structured so that it is useful to the decision maker. With information coming from multiple sources, it is not feasible or desirable to present it all at once. Instead, the information needs to be structured in a logical fashion with the appropriate level of detail in each area. Expertise, usually from a combination of in-house personnel and consultants, is needed to find the right structure for the information (issues of implementation are discussed in more detail later in the chapter).

The building blocks of an information system—the metrics and their results—must be prioritized in order to establish a logical flow of information. The metrics that are seen as the highest in value, those that decision makers rely on most heavily to understand the direction of the team and whether progress is being made toward specific goals, are known as key performance indicators (KPIs). For example, a baseball team may identify one or two hitting metrics as the most important for its offense. These KPIs should be kept easily accessible and current for the decision makers. The KPIs should be chosen carefully so that they are in line with the information that a decision maker wants most at each level of the information system.

Once the KPIs are selected, they can be layered so that decision makers can start with an overview of top-level information and drill down into different types of information or specific information sets. The starting point is often referred to as a dashboard. The dashboard for an information system exactly mirrors the function of a car's dashboard: it provides top-level information about current operations. What information is included in the dashboard is dependent upon which KPIs the decision maker wants to monitor and the specific goals of the team, but it should also be a jumping-off point for all of the other information that the decision maker needs access to. Figure 6.2 outlines one path through an information system that decision makers might follow when evaluating personnel. Starting with the dashboard, the decision makers are presented with information regarding all of the areas that they wish to monitor. The dashboard overview includes the highest-value KPIs and is also likely to include nonquantitative information, such as streaming headlines from relevant news sources or the most recent scouting reports. This dashboard is updated in real time so that the decision maker always has the most current information available.

Once the decision makers have gotten a complete view of all of the relevant information on one screen, they can start looking for information related to a specific decision. From the overview dashboard the decision makers can access the personnel dashboard, which includes a broader set of KPIs and other information focused on personnel. The personnel dashboard, for example, may highlight the performance of a particular player. Moving from the personnel dashboard to a page for a particular player, the decision makers now have access to all of the highly detailed information that the team has on this particular player.

The dashboard approach allows decision makers to easily access and explore different sets of information from two perspectives. First, they may be narrowly interested in information about a particular entity, such as a player or a team. The dashboard pulls all the information about that entity together and allows the decision maker to drill down efficiently. Additionally, if the decision makers are interested in a particular set of information, such as medical reports, then they can quickly access that through the same system.

Designing the flow of information for the decision makers requires understanding each set of information, the frequency with which it is updated, and how it is used in the decision-making process. For example, it is easy to create a system that produces information overload at the overview level, which can result in focusing on the wrong metrics, defeating the purpose of the information system. Instead, a top-level dashboard should contain only the most important, high-value information that a decision maker needs on a daily basis. There should be a logical flow to access relevant information. The information and KPIs are presented at each level of the system should be based upon the team's strategic plan, which the analyst who designs the flow of information must understand clearly.

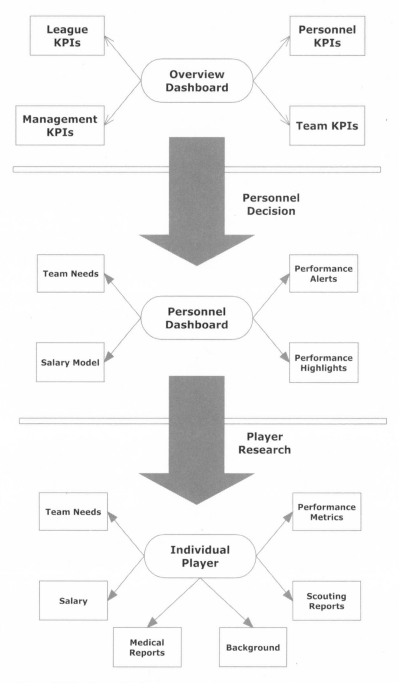

Figure 6.2 Dashboard Design

INFORMATION AND INTERACTION

Once the logical flow of the information is designed, the presentation and flexibility of the information needs to be considered. The presentation of the information influences how data will be visualized by the decision makers. Flexibility refers to the ability of the decision makers to explore and interact with the information. Both elements have significant impact on the effectiveness of an information system.

The presentation of complex information, such as quantitative performance information, is important for ensuring that the information is accessible and actionable. As an example, an NFL decision maker may need to compare the sack rates for NFL offensive lines cross-referenced by the number of defensive players rushing the QB (see table 6.1). Here the league average is presented along with information on the performance of the Dolphins and Ravens. This information can be presented in a variety of forms and is useful for making specific value comparisons, though often specific comparisons are not needed as much as a general guideline.

Figure 6.3 shows the efficient comparison of the two teams to the average, based on the number of rushers faced. With this visualization of the data, the Dolphins' sack rate when faced with six rushers jumps out as not only the highest in the data set but significantly higher than the league average and the sack rate for the Ravens in the same situation. Figure 6.3 is useful for comparing two or three teams to the league average but would become unwieldy

Table 6.1 Sack Rates by Number of Rushers

Rushers	League	Dolphins	Ravens
3	2.8%	0.0%	0.0%
4	7.1%	2.0%	4.5%
5	8.8%	4.0%	4.8%
6	4.5%	11.0%	3.1%
7	5.9%	8.0%	1.2%

and confusing if it included all thirty-two NFL teams. Altering the visualization, as in figure 6.4, however, again changes the way the information is delivered. In figure 6.4, sack rates are grouped by team instead of number of rushers. This allows the user to quickly see that the Dolphins, for example, avoid sacks better when faced with fewer rushers. The direct comparison to league average in figure 6.4 is perhaps not as clear as in 6.3, but the grouping by team in 6.4 does allow the visualization to be scaled up to include all thirty-two teams while still preserving the usefulness of the information conveyed.

This example demonstrates the importance of considering how information is presented and visualized so that it communicates effectively and serves the needs of the decision makers. There are a variety of tools that allow for advanced visualization and even basic exploration of information by the decision makers. These tools allow decision makers to intuitively explore a variety of scenarios or find deeper answers to questions inspired by top-level KPIs. Once the presentation of the information is considered, the flexibility of the system must be considered.

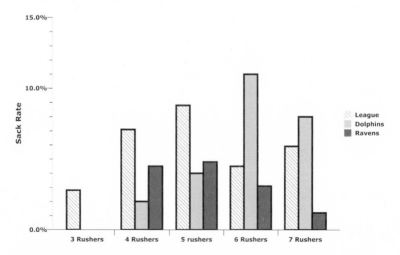

Figure 6.3 Sack Rates by Number of Rushers

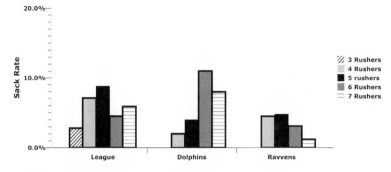

Figure 6.4 Sack Rates by Number of Rushers

Flexibility refers to the ease with which the decision makers can interact with the information. For example, an NFL decision maker is evaluating a quarterback whom he might want to acquire. However, the QB is under contract for five years, so the decision maker must consider the effects of both what the team would have to give up in trade for the player and the player's contract on the salary cap. Assuming the decision maker has a reasonable idea of what the other team would take in trade, a highly interactive information system allows the decision maker to answer these questions quickly. The information system may, for example, allow the decision maker to quickly model the move of the QB on the team's roster while moving the players traded away off of the roster, updating the salary cap model for the next five years, and projecting the effect on future wins from the roster alterations. If the information system is static, however, the decision maker must either make the alterations manually or call in the salary cap manager and statistical analyst to provide information on the new scenario. Either way, a flexible and interactive information system saves decision makers time and allows them to consider a variety of scenarios in a more efficient manner.

The information system is the tool that the decision maker uses to meld information with strategy. Designing an effective information system requires knowledge of the decision-making process, access to all of the information within an organization, and careful structuring and presentation of relevant information to maximize the time saved. When designed to be inclusive and highly interactive, the information system becomes a powerful tool that allows decision makers to be more aware of the performance of the team (both in the long and short term) and helps them analyze and explore each decision more efficiently and completely.

ADDITIONAL RESOURCES

The tools and concepts related to information systems are changing rapidly. The resources listed here provide more in-depth coverage of these tools.

Eckerson, Wayne W. *Performance Dashboards: Measuring, Monitoring, and Managing Your Business* (Hoboken, N.J.: Wiley, 2006).

Magal, Simha R., and Jeffrey Word. *Essentials of Business Processes and Information Systems* (Hoboken, N.J.: Wiley, 2009).

O'Brien, James, and George Marakas. *Management Information Systems* (New York: McGraw-Hill, 2010).

Person, Ron. *Balanced Scorecards and Operational Dashboards with Microsoft Excel* (Indianapolis, Ind.: Wiley, 2008).

Tufte, Edward R. *The Visual Display of Quantitative Information*, 2nd ed. (Cheshire, Conn.: Graphics Press, 2001).

Yau, Nathan. *Visualize This: The FlowingData Guide to Design, Visualization, and Statistics* (Indianapolis, Ind.: Wiley, 2011).

7

ANALYTICS IN THE ORGANIZATION

Innovation and Implementation

Creativity is thinking up new things. Innovation is doing new things.
—THEODORE LEVITT, ECONOMIST

Part of the value of analytics is its ability to save time for the top decision makers. But they often do not have the time to focus on and understand new metrics and the projects presented by analytics personnel, the value of which often needs more than a five-minute presentation at a meeting to be made clear to top decision makers. When building an analytics program, decision makers need to be aware of the challenge that analysts face in this regard and, in their hiring process, seek out analysts that have the ability to effectively introduce new projects into the decision-making process. Decision makers need to make sure that analysts understand this as part of their role and make sure that they can work within the existing structure of the organization and not just assume that the value they see is easily seen by others.

One NBA analyst spent a great deal of time and effort creating a new source of data to evaluate players. The analyst saw research studies that confirmed that the data had the potential to be highly valuable. For two seasons the analyst mentioned the research and the data's potential value to members of the personnel department but was unable to interest others in the project. Without support from the decision makers, the analyst saw little opportunity to advance the project. The data gathering would require both a nominal investment from the team in the form of software and the analyst's time and the involvement of the personnel to interact with the players to actually gather the data. The idea was clear, doable, potentially highly valuable, and even seemed to fit into the personnel department's general view of player value. Still, no one seemed to be interested in pursuing it, so the idea did not progress.

This set of events is not uncommon in sports or in business in general. What the analyst was trying to do was reasonable, but so was the reaction of the personnel department. Decision makers in the personnel department had not spent the time researching the ideas and theories and therefore did not share the vision of the analyst. They may have even been intrigued, but given the constant demands on their time, they do not, in general, have many opportunities to pursue new ideas. Analytics groups will consistently face this hurdle and must have effective tools for introducing new ideas, metrics, and concepts, no matter how radical, into the decision-making process.

The integration of new analytic tools and metrics into the decision-making process demands more than just including the new metrics in standard reports. One MLB analyst developed a new pitching metric that he added to a standard weekly report on pitchers that was sent to the entire personnel department. The analyst went so far as to write a detailed introduction to the metric explaining why it was being included and what information it provided about each pitcher. Three months after adding the metric to the weekly report, he got a call from a member of the personnel department who asked if there was any metric that the analyst knew of that measured a particular pitching skill. The analyst was surprised by the question because the skill was exactly what the new metric was measuring. The decision maker had no idea the new metric existed and was part of the report that he had been getting. "Oh, that's what that number is, I was wondering … great." Decision makers get used to looking at a particular set of information, and unless they are motivated to expand that set (as the MLB executive finally was), it is unlikely that they will, no matter how well the analyst makes his case in the metric's documentation. Analysts and decision makers must be aware of the adoption difficulties that new ideas and tools can face and come up with methods for the integration of analytics into decision making.

The major reason analysts fail to gain traction for their efforts is that they think like analysts. Analysts are trained to look for new metrics and build cases. They can see the deficiencies in current metrics and actively seek out improvements. Once they have developed a new and better tool, they can describe in great detail why the new tool is an improvement and how they went about building it. What analysts are not trained to do, however, is understand how nonanalysts think or engage with analysis. Analysts' working assumption is generally that if they create something new and valuable, that value will be obvious to anyone who takes the time to read the explanation.

This general approach to analytics is not without its successes. Analysts with many teams have introduced new metrics through this type of process, and some of them have been integrated into the decision-making process. This approach, however, does not give the new tools the best chance for success. Analysts need to think like innovators. The creativity and insight typical of an analyst's work is one component of innovation; finding a way to integrate the initial analysis into the decision-making process is another, equally important component of innovation.

Analysts need to recognize that part of their role is to get new and valuable information into the decision-making process, and that requires a lot more effort and planning than simply writing a memo that suggests an innovative data source or defines a new metric. It requires thinking of each new idea as an innovation that needs to be introduced carefully to the market. Here the innovation can be a new metric, a new type of data, or even some new method of delivering information to decision makers, and the market consists of the decision makers. Decision makers cannot be simply informed about new ideas; new ideas must be sold to them. Decision makers need to buy into new tools for the tools to be useful. As decision makers must be motivated to change their decision-making process, part of being an innovator is finding ways to motivate the decision makers to want to change or at least augment their established process.

Figure 7.1 Four-Phase Approach to Analytics as Innovation

CREATIVE → PROTOTYPING → ENGAGEMENT → BUILD

Analytics as innovation can take many shapes, but a fairly straightforward and effective process is for the analyst to view the process in four stages: (1) creative, (2) prototyping, (3) engagement, and (4) build (see figure 7.1). If analysts understand these four stages and plan for the entire innovation cycle from the beginning, they will maximize the probability that their new concepts will be put into practice. The depth of planning for the analyst is dependent upon several factors, including the scope of the project, the general attitude toward analytics within the organization, and the investment required in the project (in both time and money). Large projects that propose more radical change clearly require more planning, but as the MLB analyst described earlier discovered, even small additions to the decision-making process need to be introduced carefully.

The NBA analyst's project is a clear example of a project that requires some strategic planning because it requires monetary investment and ongoing action on the part of decision makers in order to collect the data. He was getting nowhere by simply suggesting the project because the decision makers had no motivation to engage with it. Once he started to think of the idea as an innovation, and not just a new data source, the analyst was able to create a plan using the four phases as a framework to get the idea put into practice.

PHASE 1: CREATIVE

The creative phase of the process is the one that analysts are typically most familiar and comfortable with. In this phase they are identifying new tools that create data, use data to create new information, or deliver information in more effective ways. The analyst is working with some combination of data, technology, and statistics to create something new that could help the organization gain a competitive advantage. This phase puts the technical skills of the analyst to the test and is where the potential for a real competitive advantage is born. For large projects, this is where analysts develop timelines and budgets, produce the supporting analysis and justification for the project, and generally work out the process for putting the project into action. For small projects, such as a new pitching metric, the analyst can often produce all of the analysis and supporting materials needed and even start including the metric in a report.

Unfortunately, this is where both the analysts described earlier initially stopped. The NBA analyst was frustrated by the lack of progress and so turned to the four-phase innovation approach in order to move the project forward. The MLB analyst, however, thought the job was complete and moved on to other projects. This is a danger of not establishing a process for the introduction of new concepts into the decision-making process. If analysts do not know that no one is engaging with their new metric, they will see the inclusion of the metric in a regular report as a success and stop there. Unfortunately for both the analyst and the organization, when the analyst stops at this point in the process, the organization has often lost an opportunity to gain a competitive advantage.

PHASE 2: PROTOTYPING

During the prototyping phase analysts build some sort of model or representation of their new tool, something that decision makers can actually engage with. The prototype can take many different forms but at its core should be something that a decision maker can see and potentially interact with that demonstrates the most important aspects of the innovation. The prototype can be a physical model, a video, a mocked-up report, or a piece of software. As the innovation has not yet been accepted as an important tool, the prototype must also be low cost (free is best) and quick to create so that the analyst is not perceived to be wasting time or resources.

When building a prototype, analysts need to consider what will engage their audience and best represent the project. Whatever the analyst builds does not have to be perfect or polished, just engaging and maybe even fun. An analyst must take care that the prototype clearly conveys the needed ideas and can motivate a decision maker. The prototype must be able to spark the decision maker's interest and should ideally be something that can be shared easily within the organization. A decision maker should be able to engage with the prototype and envision how it will help the decision-making process. This can be effected through humor, a major "wow" factor, or any other means the analyst can find.

Since the NBA analyst's innovation involved a new method for gathering data, he created a simple version of the tool through a downloadable trial version of some quiz software. And while the final version would not provide the user (the athlete) with his performance score, the prototype did. The analyst tested this prototype to make sure it delivered a reliable experience that was similar to the end product but was short and easy enough that an uninformed user could and use it instantly.

PHASE 3: ENGAGEMENT

During the engagement phase the analyst finds a way to put the prototype in the hands of a decision maker. One decision maker who has engaged with the prototype and can envision the benefits of the project will share the prototype with other decision makers. The analyst's goal is to turn the decision maker into an advocate for the innovation who will alert as many other decision makers as possible about it. If, for example, the prototype takes the form of a video, the goal is to get a decision maker to forward it on to others within the organization. As the decision makers become allies, resources become easier to come by, and as awareness and engagement among decision makers increase, so do the odds that the project will be put into practice. Awareness and advocacy from decision makers turn the question about the project from if it will be done to when it will be done.

The NBA analyst thought that the most effective way to gain advocacy for his innovation was to appeal to the competitive nature of the decision makers in the personnel group. He loaded the prototype on his computer and brought it to a personnel meeting. Predictably, several of the top decision makers were running late for the meeting so the analyst had an opportunity to get some of the more junior members of the group to take the quiz. The analyst had developed a two-sentence introduction so that anyone participating would have a basic understanding of the project's goal. As the decision makers played around and received their scores, they started comparing and competing. By lunchtime, the quiz was a major topic of discussion, which provided the analyst with the opportunity to describe the end product and the potential for valuable information in greater detail to a highly engaged audience.

PHASE 4: BUILD

Finally, during the build phase the analyst puts together the final version of the innovation that will be used by the decision makers. Here the analyst needs to make sure that the end product is practical, usable, and understood by decision makers. Additional prototyping may be necessary, depending upon the actual innovation, to ensure that decision makers understand what they are getting and how to use it. Once the decision makers (or at least one of them) are engaged then the required investment in time (from both analysts and decision makers) and money can be justified and attention to getting it "right" becomes paramount.

Part of the final build is establishing whether the innovation is actually being used. If it is, then the analyst can demonstrate the competitive advantage it delivers. If the full version is not adopted, then the analyst needs to understand why so that she can return to the engagement phase to again attempt to demonstrate the value of the project. The feedback loop can be as informal as listening during meetings to see if a new metric is being included in the discussion or as formal as monitoring use of a tool on the organization's network. Regardless of how detailed the feedback loop is, the analyst must have it in place to understand if her process was effective.

In this phase, the NBA analyst did extensive research on which software tools would provide the desired experience and data, built the quiz in the selected environment, and tested it to make sure it worked. The analyst then assisted with installing the quiz on the computer to be used in the data gathering, discussed the schedule for gathering the data with the decision makers, and checked for new data at the scheduled times. The analyst built the final project and made sure that it was being used. By employing the four-phase approach, the analyst was able to move from a promising idea to a practical tool that is now integrated into the decision-making process.

The NBA analyst's project required the investment of time and money from decision makers; the MLB analyst's project did not. After finishing the creative phase (creating the new pitching metric), the MLB analyst was able to skip to the build phase (placing the metric in a regular report) because of the nature of the project. Skipping the prototype and engagement phases, however, meant that the competitive advantage that the new metric could provide was not apparent. A prototype could have been as simple as mocked-up baseball cards featuring the new metric, which would demonstrate what the new metric could reveal about pitchers. Engagement might have involved passing out the cards at a meeting with decision makers or handing them to decision makers in a more informal setting, such as a casual conversation in the hallway, so they could examine and share them. The final build phase also needed a feedback loop. The feedback loop the analyst had delivered the clear message that the metric was not being used (the decision makers did not know it existed), but if the analyst had gone through the entire process, a few well-placed e-mails inquiring about usage from the decision makers who were most engaged could have provided the real feedback needed.

So far, the discussion of the process of innovation has focused on the role of the analyst, but decision makers have a role in this process as well. First, the decision makers need to ensure that analysts understand their role and that they are thinking about analytics as innovation. The decision makers need to think of analytics as innovation and seek out analysts who understand that as part of their role. Second, the decision makers need to be open to being sold on new tools and willing to engage with prototypes. As the culture within the organization becomes more open to innovation, the competitive advantage gained from the organization's analytic investment will grow. The role of the decision maker is to foster a culture of innovation within the organization. This includes supporting prototyping and encouraging engagement from everyone within the organization. This type of leadership is vital to implementing analytics throughout the organization to maximize the competitive advantage that analytics can provide.

IMPLEMENTING ANALYTICS

Strong leadership is needed to support the implementation of new analytics that are in line with a team's strategic goals. The benefits of analytics increase as more systems are used (as discussed in detail in chapter 9). As the systems are built, therefore, it is incumbent upon the leadership within the organization to establish the use of analytics as part of the standard best practices for making decisions. This does not mean that leaders have to base all their decisions on the new metrics established by the analytics staff or that nonanalytics personnel should lose their seat at the table in decision making but rather that the use of analytics should become fully integrated into the processes of the organization. Then the competitive advantages from analytics can be fully realized.

Each component in an analytic system grows in value with true integration into the processes of the organization. For data management, complete integration means that all data are truly centralized and that there are no data silos in the organization. From a management perspective, this is not an easy goal to achieve. Each group within the organization, particularly groups that have always held and controlled their own data, will have a difficult time transitioning to a more centralized system. Best practices need to be established so that each member of the organization understands where and how to store data to make sure that it is accessible to all. If some groups or individuals are allowed to continue to operate data silos, then some of the value of the centralization, standardization, and integration of the team's data will be lost. As data flows into the organization either through new vendors or through collection by team personnel, it is incumbent upon the decision makers to provide all members of the team with the proper incentives to ensure the inclusion of that data in the central data warehouse. This may require a shift in the culture of the organization so that data is thought of as a shared resource instead of a source of power for those that control it. Once the message of this shared resource is received and reinforced for team personnel, and they follow through by centralizing their data, the benefits will become clear. Now, instead of fielding endless requests for data that they previously controlled, staff will have more time to focus on their true responsibilities.

The integration of predictive analytics and new metrics is complete when decision makers make use of the information produced by this analysis on a regular basis and become comfortable with the value and limits of the analysis. Only through repeated use of specific metrics and regular interaction with detailed analyses of specific questions will decision makers gain the level of comfort and sophistication that is needed to fully capture the power of analytics. As different analyses and metrics are discussed and made part of the decision-making process, the organization gains two distinct benefits. The first is that the decision makers become more confident in their use of a new type of information, which helps them reduce the risk inherent in their decisions. The second benefit is that the analysis improves as the analysts get a clearer understanding of how their work is used and a more sophisticated view of the sport and the decision-making process. Initially, this repeated use of metrics and analysis must be purposeful on the part of the decision makers. They must take on the responsibility for discussing and asking questions about the work of the analyst in the context of real decision making. As questions are asked and answered, both in one-on-one discussions with analysts and in larger group meetings, all members of the team will begin to expect that this type of information will included in the discussion, and as they grow more comfortable with its use, they will likely begin to seek it out.

The consistent use of the information system may provide decision makers with the most obvious and immediate benefits because they do not have to wait for information or analysis and can spend more time analyzing decisions and less time managing sources of information. As the information system is used more consistently, decision makers will see the benefits of it in their own work, as well as in the work of the entire team. Universal adoption means that all members of the team will be accessing the same version of the truth, as discussed in chapter 2. More time in meetings will be spent in discussion when less is needed to get everyone on the same page. These benefits will continue to grow as the use of the information system becomes standard operating procedure within the organization.

The complete integration of the information system into the process of the team may be the most difficult transition for many decision makers. It requires a fundamental change in daily habits and decision-making processes. Decision makers are used to getting information from certain sources and in specific forms. Changing habits and work flows is difficult even if that change will lead to significant time savings. The transition to the use of the information system requires top decision makers, first, to provide comprehensive training and consistent support in the use of the system to all personnel, and, second, to force themselves to change their habits, for example, accessing reports through the information system rather than having printed versions and reminding others to do the same. Initially, the top decision maker's questions need to change from requests for information to requests for assistance in finding the relevant information in the system. These requests and demonstrations will lead, first, to improvements in the system as its architects learn more about how the it is being used and, second, to a greater level of comfort and ease of use. The speed of the transition from asking for information to asking for support in finding information and, finally, to efficiently accessing needed information on the fly is dependent upon both how well the system is designed and how insistent top decision makers are on its use.

Clarity about the competitive advantage created by sports analytics demonstrates the fourth tool for the analysts: leadership (figure 7.2). Fully capturing this competitive advantage is not possible without analytic leadership. In this context, no technical analytic knowledge is necessary to be an analytic leader; instead, what is necessary is the confidence that analytics can provide a competitive advantage and a general knowledge of how that advantage is realized. Once a leader can see the potential and the road to realizing that potential, then the value of analytics can be captured. The analytic leader can map analytic tools to the team's strategic plan and cultivate the use of the analytic tools within team departments. Purposeful leadership in this area is just as necessary for the success of the team's analytic investment as hiring the right personnel and establishing high-quality analytic systems. It is the leadership that will help install

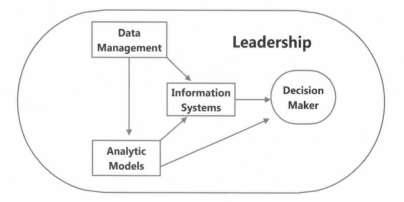

Figure 7.2 Sports Analytics Framework

analytics as a regular part of the decision-making process, which is where competitive advantage will be achieved.

INTEGRATING ANALYTICS:
THE CARDINALS AND THE DRAFT

One team that was struggling with the integration of predictive analytics in their decision making was the St. Louis Cardinals. The classic tension between scouts and analytic personnel was unfolding in the draft room as scouts protected their role in the decision-making process and were not always receptive to the work of the Cardinals' analytic group or knowledgeable about how to incorporate it into their own thinking. This natural tension created a draft-room environment in which each group (including subgroups of the scouts) argued to get "its guys" drafted instead of working toward the best interest of the team.

To solve this struggle and truly integrate all of the different types of information that were created to support draft-day decisions, the Cardinals brought in consultants in decision analysis. Using well-grounded decision-making theory, the Cardinals designed a process for their draft information that took input from every area and assimilated it into one central draft list for decision makers. The system was made clear to all groups, including how each piece of information entered the process and how it affected the final rankings. This allowed the scouts and analysts to see how they each affected the draft process and how other types of information enriched the process. All parties within the draft room, knowing that they had an effect on every decision, realigned toward making the best decision for the team. While the structure that the Cardinals put in place is not necessarily the answer for every team, each leader should consider how information types will be integrated and how to handle the potential for conflict among different groups. The most important part of that process is for each group to understand how its efforts affect the decision-making process.

8

A BLUEPRINT FOR ANALYTIC SUCCESS

Have a plan. Follow the plan, and you'll be surprised how successful
you can be. Most people don't have a plan. That's why it is easy
to beat most folks.

—PAUL "BEAR" BRYANT, FOOTBALL COACH

All teams have the same goal: win games and championships.
But the resources available and the philosophy of the decision
makers dictate that every team will have a different strategy to at-
tain that goal. In this context, a team's strategy refers to the three-
to-five-year plan that decision makers think will provide the team
with the best opportunity to achieve its goal. Decisions regarding
the allocation of resources, personnel, and in-game tactics, to name
a few, are all derived from the long-term strategy of the team. The
result is that while most teams have similar general structures (all
teams have training staffs, for example), the strength and importance of different parts of that structure vary wildly from team to
team. Within a team, the competitive advantage gained from analytics can be fully realized when analytics is used to inform and support
the team's strategy. Implementing an analytic investment with this
in mind increases the odds that the team can realize its strategic
plan.

The two main goals of sports analytics (saving time and creating
new information) are valuable to sports organizations. Each hour
saved or nugget of valuable information can lead to better decisions
by coaches, trainers, personnel executives, and the medical staff. In
fact, the more analytic tools put into place, the more valuable they

become. As analytic systems require investment in both human and financial resources, understanding how the benefits can be maximized within an organization is vital to the success of the analytic investment. In order to gain as much of a competitive advantage as possible, the investment must be made with an understanding of how the analytic tools will be built and used within the organization. While understanding that analytics has the potential to create a competitive advantage is a first step, actually implementing the tools in a way that gives the organization the best opportunity to realize that competitive advantage is vital.

INFORMING AND MONITORING STRATEGY

When decision makers implement a five-year strategy for winning a championship, they use their past experiences in conjunction with their assessment of the current team and the available resources. Consider an MLB executive hired by a small-market team as the top decision maker who is tasked with developing a strategy for winning a World Series in five years after the team has suffered through a hundred-loss season. The executive constructs a strategy based upon building a strong minor-league system that feeds talent to the major-league club and produces tradable assets. Additionally, while assessing the young prospects currently on the team and in the farm system, the executive decides specifically that the team should focus on creating a pool of pitchers to staff the major-league club and to use as trade assets to acquire offensive firepower.

The team can use its analytic resources, just as it would use its coaching and scouting resources, to give this strategy the best chance at success. Implementing an analytic strategy that is in line with this overall strategy requires attention to each tool of analytics: data management, predictive analytics, and information systems. Figure 8.1 maps major aspects from the MLB team's long-term strategy to analytic tools and concepts. There are three important elements that analytics can help support and inform: developing pitching through the farm system, identifying major-league hitters to trade for, and identifying a pitcher as either a long-term member of the staff or a tradable asset. As there are many areas in which analytics can be applied, focusing on these three elements of the strategy provides a starting point for prioritizing areas for analytic investment.

The managers of the analytic program can identify the improvements that can be made in each analytic area to support the strategy. Starting with the need to develop pitchers, data management might be improved through the organization of the data used in the draft process and on minor-league players. Predictive modeling might focus on implementing and refining draft-projection models, as well as creating models of pitching development for the minor leagues. Finally, information systems may be needed to track the performance of the minor league pitching staff so that the top decision makers can monitor progress in that area in real time.

When identifying hitters from other teams as potential trade targets, there may need to be an integration of scouting and performance data so that the decision maker can efficiently access all

	Data Management	Predictive Models	Information System
Developing Pitchers	• Draft Data • Minor League Data	• Draft Projection • Minor League Development	• Minor League Pitching Updates • Minor League Performance Trends
Identifying Hitters	• Major League Scouting Reports • Hitting Performance Data	• Hitting KPIs • Hitting Projections	• Competitor's Needs • Hitter Monitoring
Keep or Trade	• Coach's Assessment • Pitching Performance Data	• Pitching Career Curves • Pitching KPIs	• Trade Scenarios • Performance vs. Salary

Figure 8.1 Analytic Blueprint

needed information on a potential trade target. Predictive models can help identify the best KPIs for projecting future hitting performance. Finally, information systems can be developed that monitor which teams have excess hitters as well as a dearth of good pitching and report real-time updates of hitting KPIs.

The decision to trade or keep a particular pitching prospect can be supported through centralization and standardization of data related to pitching, including assessments from coaches throughout the organization and performance data from all levels of play. Predictive models can develop career projections around KPIs for pitchers. Information systems can allow decision makers to explore trade scenarios and present salary and performance projections together so that decision makers can see the long-term effect of various decisions.

In addition to supporting specific elements of the strategy, analytics can be developed to monitor its long-term progress. A detailed analysis of the strategy can establish KPIs and benchmarks for those KPIs that allow decision makers to see and clearly track the progress being made in context of the long-term strategy.

From the end goal—winning a championship—an analytics department can work backward to establish clear performance targets in various areas. For example, defining the level of pitching and hitting needed on a championship team through a set of consistent pitching and hitting KPIs establishes a consistent framework for evaluating the team and its progress. Additionally, realistic and necessary benchmarks for improvement each season can be established through historical changes in the KPIs. Finally, strategy monitoring can be built into the overview dashboard discussed in chapter 6 so that the decision maker can see whether the team is on the path toward long- and short-term benchmarks.

Strategy monitoring is highly valuable because as the team develops over the course of a season or two, it will reach certain established benchmarks and fail to achieve others. With strong strategy-support analytics, the status of the team in the various areas can be identified far more efficiently. This assists the decision makers in staying focused on the areas they have identified as priorities. Without this type of support, decision makers typically have to schedule meetings and review the performance of various areas in a more time-consuming process. Without the strategy-support analytics, any strategy-review session must begin with a detailed update on the key elements of the strategy. Once the systems are in place, however, strategy-review sessions can begin with discussion of any change in tactics necessary to better implement lagging areas of the strategy.

A BLUEPRINT FOR SUCCESS

There is, of course, no one best way to begin and develop a sports-analytics program. All teams have different structures, resources, and strategic plans. When establishing a plan for implementing an investment in sports analytics, decision makers need to have a general understanding of the tools of analytics (data management, predictive analytics, information systems, and analytic leadership) and how the combination of these tools can lead to a competitive advantage. Once the use and potential benefits of analytics are understood, the planning for the implementation of those tools to best capture the benefits is possible. There are five basic principles that an organization can use to guide the implementation of analytics. This planning procedure will help the decision maker create a blueprint for a strong analytics program that maximizes competitive advantage. The five basic principles to follow in building the program are:

1. Know the foundation
2. Think big
3. Think organizationally
4. Define the goals
5. Have no fear

As an example, consider an NBA team that recognizes the value of analytics but also understands that technology and personnel require significant investment. In order to ensure that they are making their investment wisely, they go through the following planning exercises.

Foundation

Successful plans depend on knowing the base from which the plan moves forward. Every organization has some level of data management, predictive analytics, and information systems. Identifying these allows decision makers to understand the team's biggest weaknesses (as well as potential hidden strengths). Teams can identify how each of the tools of analytics could be strengthened. This not only provides the starting point for the analytics program but also allows everyone in the organization to see how they have been using various types of data and see how improvements might help them save time and gain a competitive advantage.

The NBA team might go through this process and create the inventory given in figure 8.2. It may find that the only performance metrics that they have been using are per-game data from standard

Data Management	Predictive Analytics	Information Systems
●Central database contains scouting reports and performance data ●Separate salary database ●Separate medical database ●Training data in spreadsheets on laptops ●No standardization or integration	●Standard box score and per game metrics ●No projection systems ●No integrated analysis	●Personnel reports distributed in spreadsheet and paper forms ●Video edits transferred manually ●Coaching reports distributed only electronically ●Scouting reports sent in via direct link to database ●News gathered through a variety of Internet resources

Figure 8.2 Analytics Inventory

box scores and that the data are mostly stored in various silos around the organization, with only minimal centralization and no standardization or integration. It may find that the coaching staff has mostly abandoned paper copies of various plans and reports and that information is circulated via e-mail. Taking this inventory gives the team a clear view of where it stands from an analytic point of view.

Think Big

Once the base from which the organization will build its analytic program is established, it can be useful to brainstorm around what, regardless of resources, the analytic program could look like. With this exercise, top decision makers should think through the four fundamental tools of analytics and how different elements of each create competitive advantage for the team. Figure 8.3 provides a framework to guide the brainstorming so that decision makers are sure to think in a big and unconstrained way around all four areas in analytics while also focusing on how the intersection of these areas leads to the desired benefits. This framework allows all decision makers within the organization to identify important areas, discuss various technologies and technical opportunities, and outline how analytics might ideally affect the organization and its decision-making process.

The hypothetical NBA team could now imagine high-value information on a draft prospect's performance in a game, in the context of how his skills fill team needs, being accessed in real time from a tablet or computer. The analysis would also have links to supporting video clips. Or perhaps the team envisions an ideal analytic department that consists of three analysts with coaching or high-level playing experience and five database programmers that are on the cutting edge of data-management technology. While the precise scenarios dreamed up in these brainstorming sessions may not be realistic from a resources standpoint, allowing decision makers to envision their ideal analytic program helps to establish what they see as the most high-value pieces. For example, the NBA executive team may understand that the complete draft-information system outlined here may not be

Figure 8.3 Strategic Framework

available any time soon, but they may take the desire for that type of system as a starting point for where to build out the analytics program with the available resources. Once these ideals are established, analytics can be considered from an organizational point of view.

Organizational Analytics

Establishing and executing any analytic plan requires that analytics be thought of at the organizational level. How does information flow through the organization? How will analytic personnel fit into the organizational structure? How will the decision-making processes be affected by the incorporation of analytics? Answers to these and similar questions provide the decision makers with a clear perspective on their role as leaders in building analytics into the organization.

Our NBA team may realize through brainstorming that improving decision making around the draft is an area in which analytics could have a significant effect. Further, the executives may find in their analytic inventory that few of the team's current analytic resources have been employed to support that process. Through asking questions regarding how the use of analytics can affect processes and information flow at the organizational level, they may find that integrating background, medical, and performance data on prospects will require significant coordination among various departments that currently have little contact. Identifying these and other organizational issues allows the analytic leaders to add elements to the analytic plan that address organizational barriers.

Defining Goals

Goals for the analytics investment can be either short term or long term and either strategic or technical. Short-term goals create clear benchmarks for the analytics group and provide immediate value. These goals are often thought of as the low-hanging fruit of analytics and are most effective when they are highly visible within the organization so that all decision makers can quickly see the benefits and progress of analytics. Long-term goals may be more complex and require layers of buy-in from decision makers or the establishment of more analytic infrastructure. Strategic goals are the areas of decision making in which decision makers see the greatest potential for the tools of analytics. Technical goals involve the actual analytic tools and infrastructure that need to be developed in order to support the strategic goals.

Our NBA team might begin by establishing a list of strategic goals for their analytic investment that are in line with the idealized sce-

	SHORT TERM	LONG TERM
S T R A T E G I C	• Improve accuracy in draft • Improve in-game decision making	• Identify undervalued athletes • Increase vision into trends and meaningful events leaguewide
T E C H N I C A L	• Develop a predictive model for draft prospects • Centralize data on opponents	• Integrate video with new metrics tied to salary cap value • Establish real-time league monitoring

Figure 8.4 Analytic Roadmap

narios from thinking big, but are also specific and realistic in light of resources available. Using this list, they can then map the appropriate technical goals needed to achieve the strategic goals. The depth, cost, and complexity of the technical goals can then help sort the goals into short term and long term, creating the grid in figure 8.4.

The NBA team has identified four strategic goals for analytics: better drafting, better in-game decision making, undervalued athletes, and better vision into leaguewide trends. They have then associated specific technical goals with the strategic goals. For improved drafting, for example, they have identified a predictive model around draft prospects as a necessary step. Developing a predictive model, at least a basic model to improve the draft process, can be done in the short term (with continuous improvements planned) and without relying on large technical investments or data-management tools. The strategic goal of improved drafting can be seen as a short-term goal. The draft model has the additional benefit of being highly visible throughout the organization. All decision makers involved with the draft will use it, and the analyst that creates it will need to spend time with these decision makers to ensure that the information provided by the draft analysis is well understood and usable.

The goals, both long and short term, are developed around current resources, informed by brainstorming about ideal analytic systems and organizational impact, and give decision makers a blueprint for what should be accomplished. The goals grid allows the decision makers to see how they can phase in new analytic resources and identify where their analytic leadership will be needed most. With the blueprint in hand, the last step is for the analytic leaders to enact the plan, and incorporate the analytics into the decision-making process.

Show No Fear

Building and incorporating analytic systems into the decision-making process requires the recognition that the systems will fail. They may not always function as desired or be ready when initially targeted, and predictive models may be wrong. Recognizing these facts and moving forward anyway is what is meant by having no fear of analytics. This does not mean that decision makers should create the plan and then just close their eyes and hope for the best, but rather that once initial investments in personnel and technology are made in high level analytics, there will be a consistent tension between seeing results out of that investment and creating the best analytic systems possible. Analytic leaders must recognize the limits placed on them by time and resources and how that affects the analytic product that they deliver to the organization. They must roll out systems quickly so that all decision makers within the organization can see benefits, but they must also be ready to push forward when problems within the analytic systems arise. Ensuring that all decision makers get the information that they need, even when systems fail, is vital to the continued flow of resources to the analytic program. The danger in waiting until systems and models are perfect is that initial momentum and interest built up through the planning process will be lost and that other decision makers within the organization will have little patience for problems when they do occur.

For our hypothetical NBA team, developing a predictive model for draft prospects is one of the stated short-term goals. If the analytic program is launched in January, there would be a three-month window to create and test the draft model before the organization begins its draft analysis in earnest. If the model is not operational by the time serious draft discussions begin, then it is unlikely that the model will have any effect on the draft process. If reports on draft prospects are assembled without information from the predictive model, a structural barrier is erected that could prevent use of the model because all the other relevant information is printed and bound in a single draft book.

The three-month window to create the model, however, may force the analysts to focus on a smaller set of information. They may have to create a less sophisticated, and thus less accurate, model. The model is still useful and still reduces risk around draft decisions; it just does not consider everything that the analysts would like it to. If the analyst and analytic leaders within the organization succumb to the fear of using imperfect analytics, then the whole process will be delayed until the following year, and at least some short-term goals will not be met. This is unfortunate for the leader tasked with meeting the analytic goals and for the organization as a whole; even basic and imperfect predictive models can help reduce risk in the decision-making process. If the analysts and analytic leaders introduce the model and clearly explain the information it provides and how it reduces risk, then they have aided the organization while meeting their short-term goals. They can revise and improve the model in following years.

The process of creating an analytic blueprint and taking action on the plan with no fear gives the organization an opportunity to understand where it can reap benefits and how the organization needs to be structured to capture those benefits, and finally to demonstrate the benefits to the organization. Continued interest in the use of analytics is vital to the continued flow of resources to the program as it develops. If decision makers are not using analytic tools and seeing benefits from that use, resources will not follow. If, however, the benefits of analytics are made clear and continue to grow, then the organization will continue to embrace analytics and demand more analytic tools.

ADDITIONAL RESOURCES

The following resources discuss the issues involved with a comprehensive strategic approach to analytics and the management of an analytic team.

Davenport, Thomas H., and Jeanne G. Harris. *Competing on Analytics: The New Science of Winning* (Boston: Harvard Business School Publishing, 2007).

Davenport, Thomas H., Jeanne G. Harris, and Robert Morrison. *Analytics at Work: Smarter Decisions, Better Results* (Boston: Harvard Business School Publishing, 2010).

Laursen, Gert H. N., and Jesper Thorlund. *Business Analytics for Managers: Taking Business Intelligence Beyond Reporting* (Hoboken, N.J.: Wiley, 2010).

Stubbs, Evan. *The Value of Business Analytics: Identifying the Path to Profitability* (Hoboken, N.J.: Wiley, 2011).

9

BUILDING AND MANAGING
AN ANALYTIC TEAM

The other term was Ph.D. Poor, hungry, and driven. So he gets young
guys, he puts you in operation or he puts you wherever and then you
show that you have value, and then he may bump you up to another
department; you show you have value, he bumps you up, and then, you
know, you either survive and rise or you get cut out.

—ERIC MANGINI, FORMER NFL COACH

Once the blueprint for building and using analytics is set for a
team, the final consideration is how new analytic personnel
will be hired, evaluated, and fit into the organization. Hiring and
evaluating analytic personnel is not a straightforward exercise, and
careful thought must be put into these processes. Additionally, the
structure of the organization can affect the potential success of the
analytic investment, so fitting analytic personnel into the organizational structure also requires planning. The skill sets needed for
analytic personnel are often not precisely defined or obvious to
nonanalytic decision makers. Identifying the most important skill
sets, recruiting candidates that both have the right skill sets and fit the
culture of the organization, and then evaluating whether the hired
personnel actually performed their job well is a nontrivial process.

For example, I have visited several teams that spent significant
resources on developing their database systems. They proudly describe the process that led them to create this resource. Usually what
they have created is the first step toward a truly useful database that
makes access to their performance data easier. Unfortunately, as the
systems rarely have access to more information than can be gleaned
from websites such as basketball-reference.com or ESPN.com, it
becomes difficult to convince decision makers to actually use the

system. If the system had instead been conceived of within the full context of a sports-analytics program, then the decision makers would have access to unique information that could save them time and thus motivate them to use the new tool. Hiring the personnel that have the skills create the more comprehensive system is one of the serious challenges for leaders looking to build a sports-analytics program that delivers a true competitive advantage.

HIRING ANALYTIC PERSONNEL

I regularly receive calls and e-mails from decision makers in a variety of sports looking to hire analysts. They want to hire the best people for the job but do not know where to start looking. The hiring of analytic personnel is a different experience for most decision makers in sports because they personally do not have the skills needed to do the job and, more often than not, have not worked with anyone who does. Positions of this nature bring in a slew of applications from people of various backgrounds, but it is difficult for the decision maker, first, to evaluate what level of training the position requires and, second, to know how to evaluate the abilities of the candidates. Additionally, if the team has not gone through an analytic strategic-planning exercise like the one discussed in the previous chapter, then the posting will likely not be well defined and the interviews will eventually come to a point where the decision maker asks the candidate some version of, "So what are you going to do if we hire you?"

With extended training (i.e., graduate-level training or industry experience in analytics) come more advanced skill sets and deeper understanding of how data can be harnessed to assist the organization in gaining a competitive advantage. Additionally, requiring extended training yields a smaller pool of candidates with typically higher expectations for salary and potential for advancement. Teams must struggle with whether the more extensive skill sets and experience are worth the additional cost in salary. For most teams, the answer is that it depends upon how clear an analytic vision the decision makers have. Teams like the Houston Rockets have highly analytic people (Daryl Morey and Sam Hinkie) in top decision-making roles. Thus, the expert-level vision of how an analytics program can gain the team a competitive advantage is already in house, and such a high level of expertise does not need to come from outside the organization. Other teams, with less-analytical decision makers, may need more highly trained and experienced analytic personnel who have the vision for what the analytics program can become and have the ability to develop truly cutting-edge analytic systems.

Once a team establishes its vision for the position(s), it can start to evaluate candidates and their skills. Here the decision makers are the experts on how a particular individual fills the role and the culture of the organization. They may not, however, be experts on evaluating whether the candidates are actually able to perform the tasks that are going to be asked of them. (A question often asked of analysts in the interview process with teams is: How do I know if you are any good?) Just as scouts and coaches have various skill levels, so do analysts. If the candidate has come to the attention of decision makers through recommendations from other analytic personnel, then they can have more confidence in the candidate's abilities, but whether the candidate was a referral or not, the decision maker should work to verify the individual's analytic skills. For some candidates, this can be demonstrated through academic publications that have gone through a peer-review process to vet techniques by experts in analytic disciplines. Others require different verification processes.

One potential tool, which can then be carried over to evaluation, is to set up an internal analytic review board. The board can be a small group of analytic professionals and academics that are interested in dedicating a small amount of time to the sports industry. This group can review the established blueprint and make recommendations about the qualifications needed by candidates, then verify the skill set of potential candidates. They can even substitute for some of the broader vision and analytic experience that the organization will need, thus reducing the demands on the analytics positions. The analytic review board can then function as interested advisors to the top decision makers on specific analytic hiring and managing issues.

The Philadelphia Eagles used a structure close to this as they were ramping up their analytic capabilities. Professors from Wharton were employed to assist with the evaluation of candidates and establishing the direction of the program. The professors were able to look at work that prospective analysts had published or completed in other arenas and advise the top decision makers on whether they had the technical skills and abilities needed. This provided the decision makers at the Eagles with a built-in check on the work of their analytic staff, which helped them gain confidence in both their hiring choices and the work that came out of the analytics group.

The review board can provide another valuable service. Team analysts are often unable to discuss technical issues with anyone outside of the team, and if they are the only staff members with deep knowledge of statistics, then they are left without a sounding board to work through difficult issues and ensure that their approach is valid. The review board can not only verify that work is being done well and according to the long-term strategic plan but also serve as a resource that analysts can turn to for advice on more complex problems.

EVALUATING ANALYTIC PERSONNEL

Once analytic personnel are hired, their work must be evaluated. This poses a significant problem for decision makers with no analytic training. Consider the case of an analyst who is hired to build a model that identifies undervalued players. She may produce an analysis and even be able to discuss its context and inputs in great detail with the decision makers, but how can they, not trained in advanced statistical analysis, know whether the analyst actually did a good job? Valuing talent within the context of salary caps and luxury-tax systems is not straightforward, and the data used in the process must be treated carefully. Decision makers rarely have the experience with probability distributions that would lead them to ask the right technical questions about an analysis. Over time (perhaps four or five years) the results might validate the analysis, but, particularly with personnel decisions, which are relatively rare, it is hard to know whether a model is good and improving or just lucky. The same is true for the programmers and designers of the data-management and information systems. While decision makers interact with these systems daily, they likely are not familiar with how the data infrastructure is planned, whether it is flexible enough for future growth, or whether progress is occurring at a reasonable pace.

Here the analytic review board can serve as a useful tool. It might convene once or twice a year to review the work of the analytic personnel. The analytic review board would then function much as peer review functions in academics. It can ask questions and make suggestions to the analytic personnel and then offer a frank assessment of their work to the decision makers. The decision makers can factor the opinions and advice of the review board into their evaluation of the analytic personnel.

ANALYTIC PERSONNEL AND ORGANIZATIONAL STRUCTURE

There are three basic structural possibilities for a team's analytic personnel. The first is a centralized structure known as ACE (analytic center of excellence) in which all analytic personnel are grouped together organizationally and collectively build the team's analytic infrastructure. The second is a decentralized structure in which analytic personnel are added to existing groups so that the coaching staff, the personnel department, and the training staff, for example, all have analytic personnel working to support their needs. The third structure is a hybrid approach that mixes centralized and decentralized analytic personnel to realize the benefits of both structures.

ACE has been established in many businesses because it provides some clear organizational benefits. First, each member of the analytic group is readily available to other analytic personnel for consultation or assistance on difficult problems. This allows the analytic personnel an opportunity to push their technical approach to deeper and more informative levels. Second, a centralized group promotes standardized metrics, analytic language, and approaches to analytic problems. A more standardized approach leads to greater familiarity throughout the organization with the tools and products of the analytic group. Finally, the leader of a centralized analytics group will have the skills to take on the evaluation of the analytic personnel. This removes some of the burden for nonanalytic personnel in the evaluation process. ACE is a default organizational structure for many teams as they begin to build their analytics program by hiring only one or two staff members to begin with. If the analytics program is to become a resource throughout the organization, then the analysts must spend time reaching out to each area of the team. The San Francisco 49ers used this structure as they began to work with analytics. The centralized group provided information to both the personnel and coaching staffs. Eventually, this led to having an analyst in the booth with the coaches during games, providing analytic perspective to in-game strategy decisions.

The downside of the centralized group is that there is a natural tendency toward isolation, particularly as the group grows. When analytic personnel work primarily with one another, they are less likely to connect regularly with nonanalytic personnel. This creates two problems. First, it becomes harder for analytic personnel to increase their sports knowledge, which can make it difficult to advance their analysis. Second, without regular interaction with the analytic personnel, nonanalytic personnel will lose trust in analytics and use its tools less frequently.

The decentralized structure, in which analytic personnel are embedded into each team function, combats the isolation-related problems raised by the centralized structure. Roland Beech, for example, one of the pioneers of basketball analytics, is member of the Dallas Mavericks coaching staff. Roland travels with the team and supports the coaches. This structure allows Roland to significantly increase his basketball knowledge and see how coaches use the analysis that he provides. Additionally, since they work with him on a daily basis, the coaches have more trust in the analyses that he produces than they would if they simply found them in their e-mail each day.

The decentralized approach is appealing because analytics are used more when decision makers are in regular contact with the analytic personnel. It does, however, significantly reduce the contact that analytic personnel have with one another, which can lead to slow analytic advancement as well as a generally less consistent approach. If the analysis for coaches uses different approaches and terminology than the analysis for personnel, then the ability of the groups to communicate around analytics is diminished. This approach also generally requires a larger analytic staff so that all areas of the team can be supported.

A hybrid approach seeks to capture the benefits of both centralized and decentralized structures while minimizing their costs. In a hybrid structure, the staff of a centralized analytic group rotate through the other functions of the team. For example, an analyst may spend two months in personnel, two months with coaches, and then two months in the analytics group. In this structure, analytic personnel are exposed to the entire organization, gaining a broad perspective on the sport and how analytics can be used while still spending time with the analytics team to create standards, collaborate, and advance the technical side of the analytic work. Additionally, this approach requires a smaller group than the decentralized model because each department does not have to have its own analyst. Provided there is a centralized data resource, one analyst at a time can be "embedded" in a department while another supports the rest of the team. This type of structure still requires a larger staff than ACE, at least initially. If the Mavericks, for example, rotated Beech through various functions of the basketball organization, then some the coaches would not have consistent analytic support because the analytics group is not large enough to support all areas simultaneously.

The initial structure of the analytics group may be limited and decentralized, in that it only supports the personnel group, because the blueprint established for the analytics program starts with a small group to support personnel decisions. This is a frequent beginning for teams as the top decision makers see reluctance, for example, within coaching staffs to embrace new tools. What decision makers should recognize, however, is that as the analytics program grows and the number of analytic personnel grows with it, monitoring the structure of the group is important so that the use of analytics within the organization does not become siloed. Just as data silos reduce the value of the data, so, too, do analytic silos reduce the value of a team's analytics, wasting the investment of time, money, and effort that created them.

NOTES

1. INTRODUCTION TO SPORTS ANALYTICS

1. Jonah Keri, *The Extra 2 Percent: How Wall Street Strategies Took a Major League Baseball Team from Worst to First* (New York: ESPN Books 2011).

2. Benjamin Alamar and Vijay Mehrotra, "Beyond 'Moneyball': The Rapidly Evolving World of Sports Analytics, Part I," *Analytics Magazine* (September 2011).

3. The draft is seen as a high-value starting point because of the very public and obvious failure rate in draft picks. When players such as Matt Leinart (tenth pick in the 2006 NFL draft for the Arizona Cardinals) fail to develop into the stars that high draft picks are "supposed" to become, the failure has a large effect on the organization because of missed opportunities (Jay Cutler, for example, was drafted right after Leinart by the Denver Broncos), the financial cost of the rookie contract, and a diminished view of the organization in the eye of the public. Analytics can help reduce the error rate in the draft and so it is viewed as valuable in this area.

2. DATA AND DATA MANAGEMENT

1. Raymond R. Panko, "What We Know About Spreadsheet Errors," *Journal of End User Computing* 10, no. 2 (1998; rev. 2008).

4. PREDICTIVE ANALYTICS AND METRICS

1. None of the current top-twenty times in international competitions were recorded before 2005, and legendary U.S. sprinter Carl Lewis's best time currently ranks sixty-fifth on the all-time list.

2. Dean Oliver and Michael N. Fienen, "Importance of Teammate Fit: Frescoball Example," *Journal of Quantitative Analysis in Sports* 5, no. 1 (2009).

3. As distance from the basket increases, the shot gets harder to make. Thus, if one player shoots more long-range shots than another and if both players are equal in shooting ability, then the player with more long shots will have a lower shooting percentage.

4. The value of a shot incorporates the ability of the player to make the shot based upon the distance from the basket, the point value of the shot (two point vs. three point), and the probability that the player gets fouled on the shot (which leads to free throw attempts).

5. NEW METRICS

1. This was put to the test in an extreme case in a January 1997 game between the Lakers and Grizzlies, in which the scorekeeper intentionally gave Laker point guard Nick Van Exel as many assists as he possibly could. Van Exel totaled twenty-three assists that night, and, despite an admission from the scorekeeper that he artificially padded the assist total that night, that remains the official record of that game (Tommy Craggs, "An Assist for Nick Van Exel: How an NBA Scorekeeper Cooked the Books," *Deadspin*, August 13, 2009, http://deadspin .com/5336974/an-assist-for-nick-van-exel-how-an-nba-scorekeeper-cooked -the-books).

INDEX

ACE. *See* analytic center of excellence

Adjusted Line Yards, 50

Adjusted Net Yards Per Attempt (ANY/A), 50

Adjusted Plus/Minus, 49

analysis phase: metrics, 69–71; Player Efficiency Rating, 70–71

analytic center of excellence (ACE), 121; benefits of, 122; as default, 122; downsides of, 122

analytic models: adjusted statistics through, 8; core function of, 7; for draft selection, 7–8

analytics: coaching, 10–11; components, 4; defining, 4–5; framework, 5; goals of, 5–6; inventory, 109; investment in, 12; in organization, 10–12; other functions of, 12; player development, 12; player evaluation, 11; as process, 63–64; strategic plan and, 19, 20, 21

ANY/A. *See* Adjusted Net Yards Per Attempt

assists (basketball), 126n1; percentage, 76

Base Running Runs (BRR), 49

batting average, 48–49, 71–72

Beech, Roland, 122–23

Belichick, Bill, 52

Berra, Yogi, 44

Blair, DeJuan, 68, 71, 73–75

Boston Celtics, 7–8

box-score data, 25

brainstorming, 110–11; framework, 111

BRR. *See* Base Running Runs

Bryant, Paul "Bear," 104

build phase, 97–99

centralization, 24, 25, 27–30, 99–100; benefits of, 28–29; data quality and, 29; SAUS responses, 14, 15

centralized models: advantages and disadvantages of, 22; downsides of, 122; isolation and, 122; of personnel, 121, 122; resources use of, 22; smaller organizations

centralized models (*continued*)
gravitating towards, 23;
standardization and, 122
Cho, Rich, 33
Clarke, Arthur C., 79
Cleveland Indians, 32–33
coaches: analytics and, 10–11;
background, 53; grading scale, 54;
hiring, 52–55; risk and, 52–53;
success of, 52, 53, 54
Collison, Darren, 77, 78
communication phase, 71–75
competitive advantage, 1, 4; clarity of,
102; leadership and, 102–3;
opportunities for, 21
creative phase, 94–95
Cuban, Mark, 31
Cutler, Jay, 125n3

Dallas Mavericks, 123
dashboard: design, 86; information
system, 84–85, 86; overview, 85;
personnel, 85
data: box-score, 25; centralization
and quality of, 29; delegating
collection of, 27; flow, 4;
information differentiated from,
36; medical, 39–40; multimedia, 6;
play-by-play, 30; qualitative, 6, 36,
38–40, 42–43; quantitative, 6,
36–38, 42–43; salary, 82; scouting
reports as raw, 36; silos, 39,
99–100; types, 6; unstructured,
38, 40–41
database programmers:
qualifications, 18; SAUS
responses, 18; sport side, 17, 18
database systems, 117–18
data dependency: on one person, 15,
16, 28; SAUS responses, 16
data management, 4, 6–7; best
practices, 100; human resources,

17; implementation, 32–34, 99–100;
leadership and, 34; principles, 24,
25; resources, 34; role of, 7
data sources, 6; describing, 26;
different information from
different, 25; identifying, 26;
locating, 26; SAUS responses, 14;
standardization and, 25–26;
vendors defining, 27
decentralized models: advantages of,
22; benefits of, 123; disadvantages
of, 22; larger organizations
gravitating towards, 22–23; of
personnel, 121, 122–23
decision making: consistency in, 9; in
innovation, 99; long-term
philosophy, 19; novel insight for, 6;
results informing process of,
60–61; Saint Louis Cardinals and,
103; time saving and, 5–6
Defensive Rebound Rate (DRR), 49
depth charts, 81
Douby, Quincy, 8
Doyle, Arthur Conan, 35
draft: analytic models for selection
in, 7–8; board, 81; failures, 125n3;
projection models, 106; Saint
Louis Cardinals and, 103; Seattle
Supersonics and, 51; as starting
point, 125n3
DRR. *See* Defensive Rebound Rate
Drucker, Peter, 65
Dunlap, Mike, xi
Durant, Kevin, 36; shooting
percentage of, 37

engagement phase, 96–97
errors: automatically correcting, 30;
checking for, 15, 16, 17, 30; high
quantity of, 29; identifying, 30; in
play-by-play data, 30; SAUS
responses, 16

failure, 114
flexibility, 87, 89
Foye, Randy, 8

game charters, 25
Gates, Bill, 1
goals: of analytics, 5–6; defining, 112–14; long-term, 112; for new metrics, 65, 70; roadmap, 113; short-term, 112; strategic, 112; technical, 112, 113

heart-rate monitors, 26
Hinkie, Sam, 119
hiring: coaches, 52–55; personnel, 117, 118–20
hitter identification, 106, 106–7
hitting ability, 48–49. See also batting average; on-base percentage
Hollinger, John, 66
Houston Rockets, 25, 119
Hudl, 4
human resources investment, 17; data management, 17; time saving through, 17. See also personnel
hybrid models, 22; benefits of, 123; of personnel, 121, 123–24

ICE. See Interactive, Collaborative, and Evaluation system
implementation, 99–103; basic principles, 108; of data management, 32–34, 99–100; leadership for, 99
information: data differentiated from, 36; data sources and different, 25; flexibility of, 87, 89; flow design, 85; interaction and, 87–90; levels, 83–85; multiple sources of, 84; player, 83; presentation of, 87; risk trade-off, 51; sets, 82–85; visualizing, 88

information systems, 8–10; advanced, 10; building blocks of, 84; complete integration of, 101–2; components of, 79; consistency in, 101; constructing, 79; dashboard, 84–85, 86; designing, 17; efficiency of, 79–80; estimations, 9–10; at high school level, 10; interactive component of, 9; magnet board, 80–82; prioritizing, 84; resources, 90
injuries, 31
innovation: actual use of, 97–98; build phase, 97–99; creative phase, 94–95; decision making role in, 99; engagement phase, 96–97; feedback loop, 98; four-phase approach to, 94; investment in, 98; prototyping phase, 95–96
intangibles, 47
integration, 7, 24, 25, 30–32, 41–43, 42; of information systems, 101–2; injuries and, 31; of metrics, 92; synergy from, 31
Interactive, Collaborative, and Evaluation system (ICE), 82
Internet, ix–x
interns, 27–28
interviews, 50
inventory, 26; analytics, 109; constructing, 26; definitions laid out in, 26; standardization, 26

Johnson, Jimmy, 52

Karl, George, xi
key performance indicators (KPI), 84, 107
Krossover Intelligence, 4

leadership, 5; competitive advantage and, 102–3; data management and, 34; for implementation, 99; limits, 114

Leinart, Matt, 125n3

Levitt, Theodore, 91

Lewis, Carl, 126n1

Lombardi, Vince, 52

long-term goals, 112

Ma, Jeff, x

magnet board: grouping on, 80; limits of, 80–81; maintaining, 80; privacy and, 81; replacing, 81–82; setting up, 80

Mangini, Eric, 117

medical data, 39–40; as unstructured data, 40

metrics: analysis phase, 69–71; communication phase, 71–75; context of, 72; creation model, 69; descriptive, 70; documentation, 70; evaluating, 70; example, 49–50; four-phase process of, 65, 66; goal established for new, 65, 70; integration of, 92; interpreting, 71; opportunity phase, 66–67; passing, 75–78; predictive, 70; previous attempts at, 67; private, 66; public, 66; questions about, 66; refining, 66; scale of, 72; successful, 66; survey phase, 67–69; testing, 69–71; value of, 71. *See also* innovation; *specific metrics*

MIT Sloan Sports Analytics Conference, 37

Morey, Daryl, 31, 119

multimedia data, 6

name repetitions, 27

New England Patriots, 7

Oakland A's, 1–2

OBP. *See* on-base percentage

obstacles, 2

Offensive/Defensive Efficiency Rating (OER/DER), 49

offensive rebounding, 56

Oklahoma City Thunder, 33

Oliver, Dean, 47–48

on-base percentage (OBP), 48

one version of truth, 9, 29, 101

opportunity phase, 66–67

organizational structures, 21–23, 111–12; personnel and, 117, 121–24

Orlando Magic, 80

pass-blocking ability, 57–58

passing metrics, 75–78

pedometers, 26

PER. *See* Player Efficiency Rating

personnel: centralized models of, 121, 122; dashboard, 85; decentralized models of, 121, 122–23; embedded, 122–23; evaluating, 117, 119, 120–21; hiring, 117, 118–20; hybrid models of, 121, 123–24; organizational structures and, 117, 121–24; recommendations, 119; skill sets, 117; training, 118; verification process, 119; vision for, 119

Philadelphia Eagles, 7, 120

pitcher development, 106

Pitch F/X, 2

play-by-play data, 30

player: capabilities, 12; development, 12; information, 83; intangibles, 47

Player Efficiency Rating (PER), 66; analysis phase, 70–71; distribution for centers and guards, 74; improving, 73; scale of, 73; survey phase, 67

player evaluation, 21; analytics, 11; standard, 11
point guard, 51
Pollard, William, 24
Portland Trailblazers, 7
predictive models, 106–7
Presti, Sam, 33
privacy, 81
prototyping phase, 95–96

QBR. *See* Total Quarterback Rating
qualitative data, 6, 38–40; forms of, 36; general attitude towards, 39; handling, 39; processing, 39, 40; quantitative data combined with, 42–43; quantitative data separated from, 38; as unstructured data, 38
quantitative data, 6, 36–38; forms of, 36; qualitative data combined with, 42–43; qualitative data separated from, 38
quarterback time to throw, 58
question asking, 46–52; analyses, 55–63; at beginning, 56–57; context of result, 57–58; metrics, 66; thought process, 56–57; uncertainty, 58–60

Reid, Andy, 52
review board, 119–20; evaluations by, 121; as sounding board, 120
risk: hiring a coach and, 52–53; information trade-off, 51; reducing, 50; scouting reports and, 50. *See also* uncertainty
Rondo, Rajon, 8
Rose, Derrick, 77, 78

sack rates, 87, 87–88, 88, 89
SAFE. *See* Spatial Aggregate Fielding Evaluation

Saint Louis Cardinals, 7; decision making and, 103; draft and, 103; tension within, 103
salary data, 82
sample size, 58
San Antonio Spurs, 1–2
San Diego Padres, 7
San Francisco 49ers, 122
SAUS. *See* Sports Analytics Use Survey
scouting reports, 25; comments in, 47; nuances in, 41; as raw data, 36; risk and, 50; standardizing, 40; structured, 38
Seattle Supersonics, 32–33; draft pick, 51
short-term goals, 112
shot value, 126n4
Spatial Aggregate Fielding Evaluation (SAFE), 49
Splitter, Tiago, 68, 71, 73, 74–75
Sports Analytics Use Survey (SAUS), 2, 3, 13–14; centralization responses, 14, 15; database programmers and, 18; data dependency responses, 16; data source responses, 14; error responses, 16; results of, 21; statistical analysts and, 19, 20; strategic plan responses, 20
SportVu, 37
sprinter, 44–45; medal-winning time, 45; progress of, 45, 45–46
standardization, 24, 25; centralized models and, 122; challenges, 26–27; data sources and, 25–26; inventory, 26; player evaluation, 11; of scouting reports, 40
statistical analysts: evaluating, 18–19, 20; qualifications, 18; role of, 17; SAUS responses, 19, 20; on sport side, 17–18, 19

Stats LLC, 37, 82
Stokes, Sean, 10
strategic goals, 112
strategic plan: analytics and, 19, 20, 21; SAUS responses, 20; supporting, 21. *See also* team strategy
survey phase: metrics, 67–69; Player Efficiency Rating, 67

Tampa Bay Rays, 1–2, 24
TAv. *See* True Average
team chemistry, 47–48
team strategy, 104; blueprint, 108–16; foundation of, 109–10; informing, 105–8; monitoring, 105–8; supporting, 106
technical goals, 112, 113
technology investment, 32–33
time saving, 91, 104–5; decision making, 5–6; through human resources investment, 17; new metrics for, 65
Total Quarterback Rating (QBR), x, 50
training, 118

True Average (TAv), 49
true value, 59

uncertainty: questions about, 58–60; reducing, 61–63; types, 58
United States Olympic Committee (USOC), 44–46
universal adoption, 101
unstructured data: analysis of, 40–41; medical data as, 40; qualitative data as, 38; structure imposed on, 40–41; time investment with, 40
USOC. *See* United States Olympic Committee

Van Exel, Nick, 126n1
variability: comparison of, 59; importance of including, 60; measuring, 58–59; sample size and, 58
video, 25; context level in, 57; structuring, 40–41

Westbrook, Russell, 75–78
Woolner, Keith, 33